Småland gave birth to me
I was travelling through Sweden
Watched the bowels of the earth 450 ells deep
Rose in the wind's heights about one mile
Watched summer and winter on same day
And spent that day therein
Perambulated clouds
Visited the end of the world
Watched the sun's night shelter
In a year's time walked 1000 miles
On land.

Carl von Linné

**For Niklas,
my incomparable son**

...just till over there!

Trekking round the Arctic Circle in Swedish Lapland

by

Klaus Heyne

Important note:

Triggered by the wish to make my travel experience available even for overseas readers, I translated the text part of this book from German to English by myself.

As English is not my mother tongue I would like to apologize in advance for any confusion resulting from translation errors.

Please be gracious! If you find any hair-raising mistakes, don't hesitate to contact me by email (*see last page*) and provide me corrective indications for not letting me die stupid.

Copyright © 2014 Klaus Heyne
Volume 2
Manufactured and published by Books on Demand GmbH, Norderstedt
ISBN 9783735778499

Bibliographical data of the Deutsche Nationalbibliothek (German National Library)

The Deutsche Nationalbibliothek lists this publication in the Deutsche Nationalbibliografie; detailed bibliographic information is available online at http://dnb.d-nb.de

...just till over there!

For a moment I was with you
rested for a while

And now my friend, my dear bird
it is time to leave again
It is always like that towards the end

And I take out the white reindeer fur coat
not so new any more
but not worn either
And I take out the mottled fur shoes
new shoe strings
nice dark fur leggings
the silver belt the gákti
the silk scarf the cap
the fur gloves
And the food pack

I leave
to arrive
go away
to be closer

To the space of your thoughts
to your heart
I crawl
into the heart

I journey
on the sea of time
follow
the tracks of the wind

Nils-Aslak Valkeapää [Valkeapää1]

...just till over there!

Klaus

Niklas

Jens

...just till over there!

Table of Contents

...just till over there!

...just till over there!

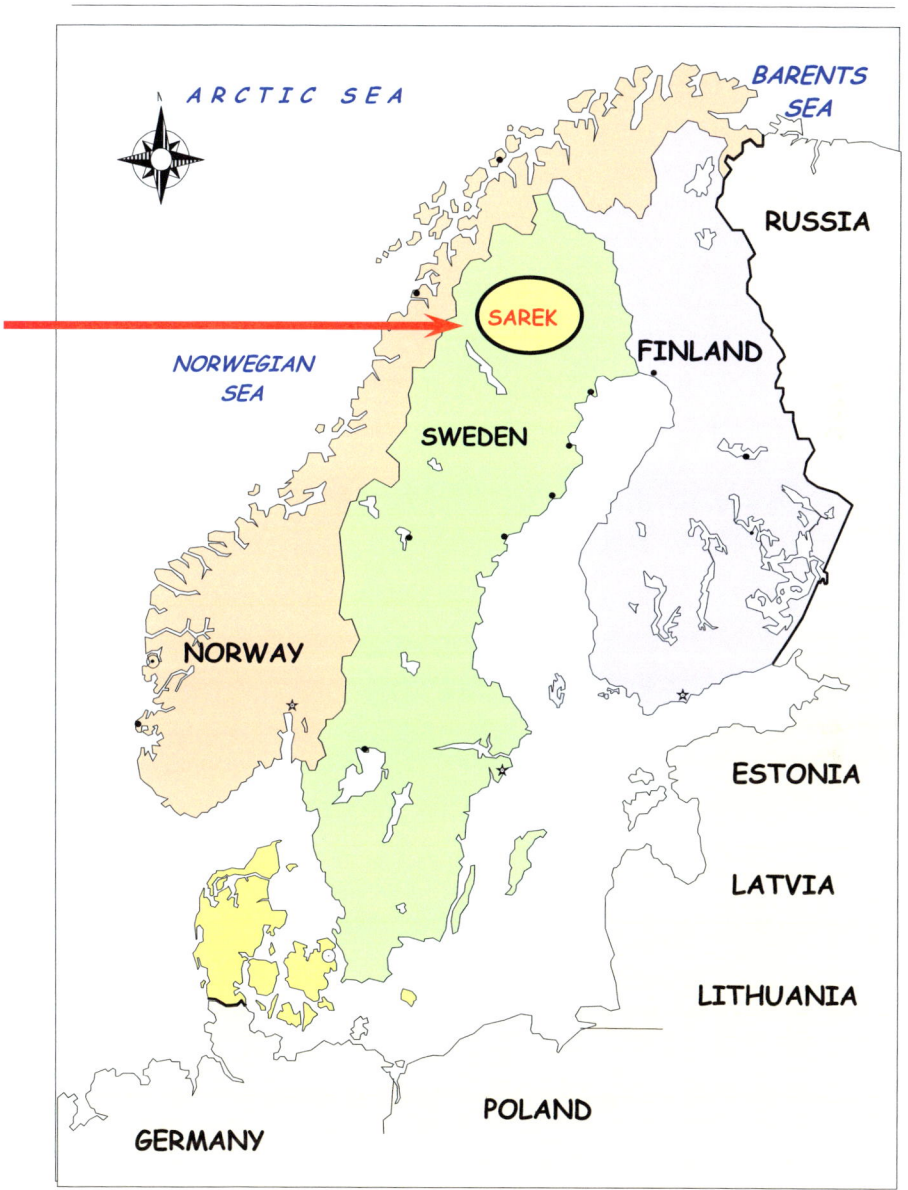

...just till over there!

Realized Route 2012

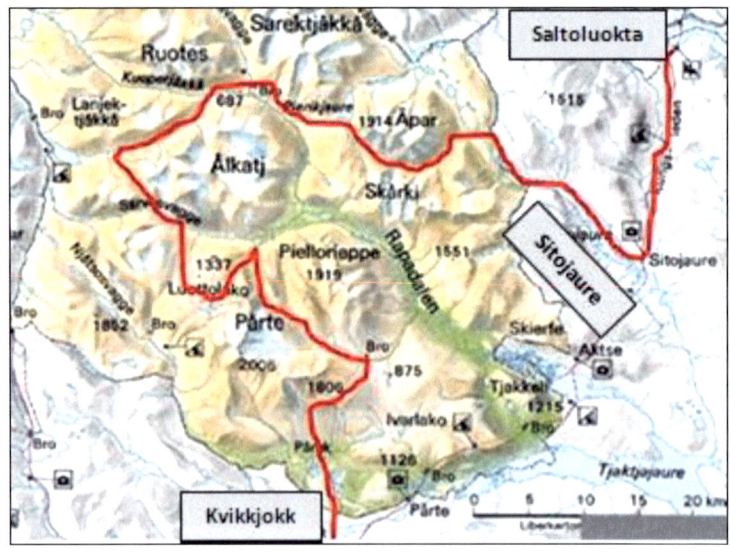

Planned Route 2012

...just till over there!

Why, oh why again to Lapland?

This question can only be asked by someone, who was not (yet) touched by the charm of the Far North. Possible yes, but difficult to imagine for me.

Those, who are suckers for merely endless vastness without any streets, roads or other achievements of civilizing is in good hands here. The abundantly sung about credo „back to the roots" will be happen right in front of your eyes. A walking tour, i.e. to experience a landscape by own physical effort, means a complete

> *It was only beyond the hotels and the paved ways, the real Lapland was stored for us. But most of the tourists will never learn about this treasure for free, handicapped by their luggage and their need for comfort. Instead of walking through the open door the arctic offers them, they like it more to get in the car and will bring back home only a few crumbs of the polar endlessness.*
>
> *[Crottet2, pg. 21]*

different experience than to reach (travel) destinations by usage of comfortable aids (e.g. chairlift to the Alpine peak).

Only the fact to be on one's own separates the wanderer in „the wilds" from the common tourist. One learns to scale down his needs and to concentrate on the basics. One will be happy, if the sleeping bag remains dry and the pot is warm and well-filled. The total abstinence from all these things that affect us bugging and oppressing in a hundred different kinds every day (phone, TV, road traffic, ...) clears your mind and gives all the feelings you get on such a journey an intensity that an all-inclusive package holiday will never bear.

In this context I do not grow tired of quoting the German cameraman Dietrich B. Sasse, who said in the 1950ies: „*Who once was wandering in Lapland, fell under its spell. The only way to break the spell is to return.*"

> *In the great silence of the polar world, in view of the northern lights it will be tangible to man, that there are powers beyond his individual reality controlling and directing his life.*
>
> *[Crottet1, pg. 15]*

And Robert Crottet wrote: „*I have travelled to nearly all countries of the world, but only here I found something like a little paradise*". *[Crottet1, pg. 13]*.

And that's it, why it must be Lapland again.

But this time there is another good reason for choosing especially this travel destination. My dearest wish came true. Niklas, my 17-year-old son, will be with us. I'll jump for joy to share truly my rage for this kind and destination of travelling with him and to let him experience the land beyond the northern polar circle with the peculiarities of the Arctic. Be it the phenomenon of the midnight sun or endless fields of boulders and trackless birch tree forests or mosquito pestilential swamps or eternal snow on the mountain tops. – I hope, the unique nature, Hamsun's *"Totality of Nature"*, will make his presence felt and channel his desires on the actually important things. Even if – or even then – one will go outside the envelope and will bring himself to continue walking – *... just till over there!*

*

During all those years being in the northern lands, I often recognized that people living in Middle European latitudes, actually were not able to class Lapland geographically. At school, one usually does not come across that area. I remember just a single mention of Lapland in geography lessons in the first or second class of grammar school, when the teacher talked about ore mines in Kiruna. Indeed, there is no greater public or political interest in that

> *„Lapland donates everything and demands nothing." But that is incorrect. It is not true, that Lapland does not demand anything. On the contrary, it demands a lot, namely no less than a kind of suicide. One ought to put off that self brought from the so-called civilized countries and drown it in the Lake Inari (…). It didn't take long when I discovered that I couldn't teach them [the Laplanders] anything. With hardly recognizable irony they made it clear, that they were the teachers and that my whole intellectual luggage weighed much too light. When they did not know Shakespeare nor Goethe, Rembrandt or Bach, it was not important for them. All around them and within them, there was music, poetry, painting. They need not to be creative, because they were so close to creation.*
>
> *[Crottet2, pg. 22]*

country. Even the media coverage about the radioactive cloud of Tschernobyl at that time, which was reason for the emergency slaughter of thousands of reindeer, did just run to the mention of the Gulf of Bothnia. Everything else was only named "further north". Well, anyway, Lapland is not a sovereign state with commonly accepted national borders, but the living space of an ethnic minority, that spans over the northern regions of Norway, Sweden, Finland up to the Russian Kola Peninsula. An area, that reaches up to the Norwegian Sea and where the Arctic Circle belongs to the south.

...just till over there!

Who is going to deal with that subject will inevitably be confronted with the terms *Arctic*, *Lapland*, *Sapmi*, *Sami* and *Nordkalotte*, which must not be used synonymically and might lead to confusion. *Lapland* in a strict sense only includes the Swedish landscape (landskap) Lapland (an administrative province till 1634) and Finland's northernmost province Lapland *(Lapin lääni)*. The Norwegians exactly regard these two provinces as Lapland. It is uncommon to use the term Lapland for the Russian Kola Peninsula, either.

In distinction from that there is the actual settlement zone of the *Sami*, the Lapp natives, namely *Sápmi*, which reaches far beyond the historical Swedish province Lapland from their point of view. Even though the Sami have been forced back on and on to the North during the last centuries, today *Sápmi* spans from the Kola Peninsula down to Idre in the (middle-) Swedish province Dalarna and Engerdal in the Norwegian district Hedmark.

On the other hand, the term *Nordkalotte* identifies the northernmost regions of the Scandinavian Peninsula around the Arctic Circle and the area north of it.

The region of the *Arctic* is defined by climatic criteria: for example the treeline or the July-isotherm of $10°C$ are normative for the delimitation of the areas in the southern regions of the earth. In former times the Arctic was simply determined as "Area north of the Polar Circle" *(66°33´ latitude north)*. However, the climatic zone of the Arctic is not restricted by the polar circle.

If Nils Holgersson would fly once again on the back of the grey wild goose Akka of Kebnekaise high above her home, he would see in the far west the high mountains of the *Skanden* (Scandinavian Mountains) covered with glaciers and a coastline rugged by hundreds of fjords. He would see in the eastward of the mountains a tundra like plateau, interveined by swamps and rivers. He would see vast boreal forests, which spread from the plateau deeply into the valleys.

One can process these mere facts with a geographical basic knowledge and compare it to the world map before his mind's eye. That's no problem. But it will be much more difficult to clarify the vast extent, loneliness and nativeness of the landscape. For many of us the lack of streets or other infrastructure is totally unimaginable. I often heard remarks as: „ *Well, if you get tired, you can walk to the next highway and hitch a ride to the next village"*, which is the expression of a standard idea of a landscape. My response to that explaining that there are no highways, no villages, regularly will not really reach my counterpart. One will recognize his vacant expression showing it clearly. This imagination is that far away from his empirical world that his brain refuses to accept such unimaginabilities. The non-presence of towns and villages falls into the same category.

Tell someone of your circle of friends and acquaintances, you were walking about seven days in one direction and you didn't meet any other person, didn't see any road, any house or power pole – and then pay attention to his face…

Then you will surrender, going into raptures over the beauty of the endless vastness, making him understand why an infertile valley, full of shredded leftovers of former mountain tops can be fascinating. Why it is worth to experience walking on physically extremely demanding paths.

He will never understand and of course will not be able to do so as far as he will not have first-hand experience thereof. Sometimes it needs an outer initial push. Even today I am delighted about my friend Oliver, having a lasting effect on me in this affair.

> **Can you hear the sound of life**
> **in the roaring of the creek**
> **in the blowing of the wind**
> **That is all I want to say**
> **that is all**

Nils-Aslak Valkeapää [Valkeapää2]

...just till over there!

Sunday, July, 15th:
Arrival

In the last days I thought and thought of the northland summer's perpetual day.

[Hamsun, pg. 869]

Ready at last! The recent weeks had been filled with a thrill of anticipation and sweat-soaked test runs through the woods of Göttingen and the Elfringhauser Schweiz (near Hattingen in the Ruhr Area) carrying a 30-kg-piece of backpack. This period came to an end today. Instead of this begins the worrying about the successful convalescence of about only 14 weeks after my knee surgery (arthroscopy), i.e. was this recovery phase sufficient for the coming operation?

Nevertheless: the day of departure is now! The plane will take us from Düsseldorf to Stockholm. An additional domestic flight will carry us to Gällivare, which is an urban treasure within the natural site **World Heritage Laponia**

Sonni kicks her boys (husband and son) out at the departure terminal and Niklas and I move the jam-packed baggage cart in the full to overflowing check-in area, where at least 200 persons/families are queuing fanhold – and all of them are ahead of us. There are only 30 minutes left until the end of the boarding time. We will never make it!

But the routine of the dispatchers enables us having even 5 minutes in reserve. Thus, we can stroll to the gate without a hurry.

Check-in, fly off and land in Arlanda, Stockholm's airport. We are going to meet Jens here, who will be arriving from Zurich. Asking the lady at the information desk for some news about the plane from Switzerland, we learn that it landed just a few minutes ago. Niklas and I detect the right gate for departure to Gällivare in the meantime and are still waiting for our so far missing friend. Even using a strategically significant point does not help. But he does not appear. In addition to that we didn't get any answer to several SMS's.

„Son, I'm afraid the Swiss confederate missed his plane. He doesn't answer not at all!"
„Nonsense, he is going to come to light! Listen to me!" my optimistic offspring argues.

And thus it happens. At 10:30 h he passes by, maundering at an idle speed and meets us anywhere on the airport area, where we had changed our position many times in the meantime.

...just till over there!

As things turn out, he has some problems with his luggage. The rod system of his trolley, which had to be checked in as a separate item of luggage, was not on the baggage conveyor belt after landing in Stockholm. That is why he had an odyssey to the counter of SwissAir and the information desk andandand in the meanwhile. Alas, without any success.

Jens found something in the internet that appears to his mind as a serious alternative to the classical backpacking: namely a vehicle similar to an Indian sledge, but having a wheel at the end. This construction needs to be fixed to the body by means of some harness and to be dragged behind oneself. He expects a vast relief for the back of using it. For this purpose he reconstructed a mountain bike trailer and tested it in the Swiss mountains. And he found it good. One part of the trolley is just the drawbar, which consists of two aluminium tubes – and these ones are missing now.

Jens and his trolley

It is time now to check in for the domestic flight to Gällivare. At the counter we ask the lady on duty for the missing tubes - but no success again. They remain undiscoverable. Only Jens's backpack is present. May be the tubes will arrive with next plane? Nobody knows. Jens is to call the airport in Gällivare in the evening. Probably there will be new details in this affair.

Well, we want to stay overnight in Gällivare anyway. I booked a small cabin on the local camping ground beforehand. The worldwideweb makes it possible.

Gällivare – a small town, yes, yet still one of the biggest in the northern region – is in the northern Swedish province *Norbottens Län* resp. the historical province *Lappland* and 70 km north of the Arctic Circle.

The Arctic Circle is determined by the latitude of 66° 33', where the sun reaches the highest meridian altitude on the day of the summer solstice (June, 21st). That means that the sun is in full view for 24 hours a day. The duration of this spectacular period increases, the farther north one goes. At the Arctic Circle this phenomenon can be watched roughly said between June, 12th and July, 1st at the North Pole between March, 20th to September, 23rd. That is not to say, that at the Arctic Circle there will be complete darkness beginning with the 2nd July. Starting July 6th the upper edge of the sun disappears behind the horizon – but there will be twilight

---

*Their **Moxa** is made of a fine fungus found on the birch, and always chosen from the south side of the tree. Of this they apply a piece as large as a pea, upon the afflicted part, setting fire to it with a twig of birch, and letting it burn gradually away. (...) It produces a sore that will often keep open for six months afterwards, nor must it be closed till it heals spontaneously. This remedy is used for all aches and pains; as the headache, toothache, pleurisy, pain in the stomach, lumbago, &c. (...) It is the universal medicine of the Laplanders (...).*

***Kattie** is a kind of drawing or ripening plaister (...): the fine loose scaly bark of birch is set on fire, and immediately quenched in water. It is then chewed, (...) and afterwards mixed with fresh turpentine from the spruce fir, both being kneaded together by the hands, till the mass becomes a black uniform plaister. This (...) is successfully applied to hard imposthumes, &c.,(...).*

*An **ointment for burns** is made of fresh cream boiled to a thick consistence, with which the sore is anointed. It removes the pain, and admirably promotes the healing of the ulcer.*

*For chilblains, the oil or fat which exudes from toasted **reindeer cheese**, rubbed upon the part affected, is a sovereign cure. Some persons use **dog's fat** for the same purpose. The latter is also used for pains in the back, being rubbed in before a fire.*

[Linné1, pg. 275f]

---

from dusk till dawn. Darkness will set in as we go along.

Gällivare has about 8500 inhabitants, a historical train station and a hospital – of which more later.

...just till over there!

Jens and I start at the camping ground, looking for something we can waste for dinner – during the taxi ride from the station to the camping ground we passed a supermarket that is opened today, on a Sunday up to 22:00 h. One of the two cash machines in Gällivare, oh well, even here at the last toehold of civilization you find them, doles out a dose of money, that will be converted into bread, sausage and spaghetti the next minute.

Meanwhile Niklas nurses his right foot. Only 3 days before leaving to the wilderness someone of his comrades poured nearly boiling water thereon with the result that a hefty burn blister spreads over two of his toes (diagnostic analysis: second-degree burn).

At home our Doc made an expert job on curing the wound and handed us a wide range of things for taking care of it, when we would be on the road (e.g. gauze, desinfectant, Betaisodona, aspirins, mull, tape). One will not find all of this medicine in nature (*see text in the box above*).

Back at the hut, Jens contacts the airport again. Again, no news on that topic. Jens girl-friend Sabine contacted the airport in Zurich and got to know, that the rods have left Zurich anyhow and thus must lie around somewhere at the Stockholm Airport. Probably some kind of jackass put them into a corner somewhere and forgot it afterwards.

There is need to ask again in Stockholm tomorrow in the morning. That means, that we will not take the bus at 9:50 h, but the last one at 13:50 h, if the package actually will arrive with the midday-plane.

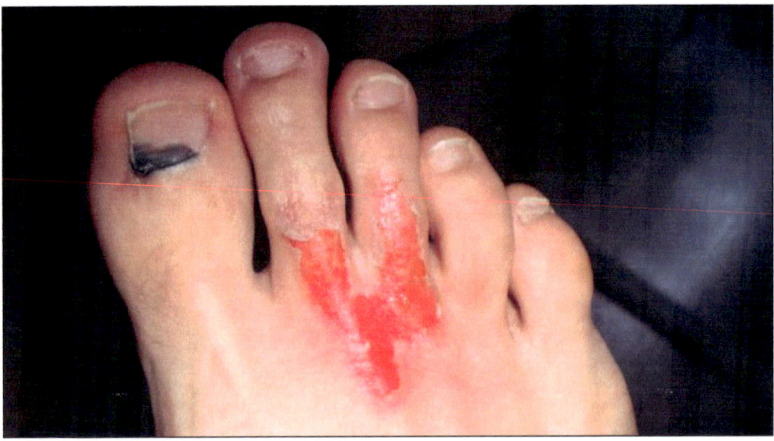

Niklas's Burn

...just till over there!

Day 1 | July, 16th:
Complications

The hut is stuffy and warm. Therefore it is no good idea to shut the window. On the other hand, this allows free access to the mosquitos, to which we have our first closer contact here.

> *The trees here produce Usnea arborea (Lichen plicatus), which the Lap-landers apply to excoriations of the feet caused by excessive walking. They line their shoes with this moss, a practice which might with ad-vantage be adopted by soldiers on a march. The Laplanders also line their shoes with grass, consisting of various species of Carex. This grass they comb with iron or horn combs, bruising it between their hands till it becomes soft and pliable. When dried they cram it into their shoes, and it answers instead of stockings for defending the feet from cold.*
>
> *[Linné1, pg. 260]*

Early in the morning Niklas wakes me, standing totteringly near the bunk bed, from which I chose the upper part last evening.

„I think, there is something wrong", he murmurs, staggering 3 paces in direction to the living room and collapses there. He is unconscious for some seconds. His forehead shows some bulbs that might be caused by bug bites.

While Jens keeps an eye on Niklas, I am running to the reception gathering for help. As it is quite early in the morning nobody is there.

An older Swedish woman is sitting on the front porch of another guesthouse that is close to the reception building. Drawing closer to her, I ask for a doctor. I can communicate with her as she has a few scraps of English available and she dials the emergency call on her mobile phone. She tries to explain something to someone, but as she doesn't know any details, she handed the phone to me so can I speak to a lady at the other end of the phone

All this takes quite a while and as I do currently not know how Niklas is doing at the moment, we agree on a pickup by ambulance car. But this may take a while, depending on the availability of the vehicle.

In the meantime, the husband of the Swedish woman has appeared on the scene (only speaking Swedish) and tells me gesticulating, that he can drive us to the hospital. That is the local SJUKHUS – tcha, that's the way how to learn foreign words.

The connection to the emergency central is still up and thus, I unsubscribe the ambulance car and declare we will get to the hospital by our own. I lead the way to our hut, where the kind Swede is going to give us a lift. My son lies on the bed and obviously his condition has increased in the meanwhile.

As things turned out, the hospitals is just round the corner – less than 3 minutes car drive from the camping ground. We thank our chauffeur and go to see the emergency department.

Sister Amanda takes care of us and our names and addresses and sends us to the waiting area. Niklas looks quite normal again and feels so, too. Well, as we are here now, I think it best to clarify the situation. The morning bus has left anyway and thus, Jens has room enough to worry about the shaft of his trolley.

The SJUKHUS presents the northern dogtrot by its best. We were upgraded and are now sitting in a treatment room, waiting for the doctor in charge. A moment after he appears in the shape of a junior doctor, radiating a dynamic like a ten-pack valiums. But he is of the kind sort and actually wants to help. His name is Anton, as he introduced himself, writes down all we argue beginning with the overheated hut, the "forehead bulbs", the burn blister, the sack full of medicine for Niklas's foot up to the fact, that a situation like today happened once before 2 years ago. At that time my son suffered from a heavy cold in coincidence with projectile nosebleeding, which awful sight kept him tossing down sidewards remaining unconscious on the floor. Anton asks some questions for eliminating some ambiguity here and there, notes the patient is visibly well and concludes the reason for our troubles must be a mental overreaction. The only confusing thing for him is the accompanying unconsciousness. This circumstance is, what he wants to discuss with a senior colleague.

Jens is on the phone for hours and confers with the Swedish airports. After all, successfully. Lastly they found the alu rods somewhere in the Stockholm Airport – Heureka! – and they have been tacked onto the wings of the first plane that left Stockholm for Gällivare this morning. After information from the *flygplats* they will be carried by taxi to the camping ground and in addition to that, the taxi driver is said to take us to the railway station, where the bus to Saltoluokta will leave, too.

Anton is back. As he wants to be sure that there will be no bad surprise during our expedition, he likes to take an EKG of Niklas's heart. Just spoken this, an assistant is rolling the machine in and plugging Niklas professionally.

The electronic expertise provides a solid result. All curves are pretty rhythmic and within normal limits. Anton nods satisfied, serves us with a handful of antihistamines against possible overreaction to further insect bites and demobilizes us with a passionless, friendly face.

We return to the camping ground by foot, trespassing the terrain of „Old Gällivare", a small museum village, which is situated in direct neighbourhood of the camping ground.

Jens informs us shortly about the new situation concerning the rods. There is enough time left, to collect our things and wait for the taxi.

At last, it actually arrives in time. The rods lie in the car trunk, which is going to be filled up to the edge with our backpacks. The taxi driver is an earthy guy, blessed with a voice that seems to be hovering over the wall of a chest clinic. A blithe spirit – loud, jovial, likeable.

It is a short way to the station – not more than 5 minutes. While driving down the street to the station, the driver praises the sightseeings of his town with widely spread arms croakily and stertorously: „Traiiin Station – headquarter of local alcoholics!"

*

A 2-hours-busdrive follows that brought us to the landing stage Kebnats at the shore of the lake Langas, which is not more than the eastern lengthening of the giant catchment lake Akkajaure. On the way there was just one further stop in the village Porjus. Up to now there was plenty blue sky and sunshine, that enlightened three times the scenery, when a lonely reindeer padding slowly ahead of the bus, keeping him breaking as long as it is graciously willing to leave the asphalt way and vanish in the bushes besides the street. I wonder, how many reindeer we are going to see in the mountains. Or other wild animals as bears, wolves, lynxes and wolverines. Some of them appeared in larger numbers in the last years.

In the numerous lakes and along the long coastlines, there are many fresh- and saltwater fish, but also seals and beavers splashing about in the water here. Whereas the number of *species* of fish is small – in contrast to the species of birds. Anyhow many migrating birds visit this region for the reason of sitting on eggs.

In addition to that one estimates that about 1.000 species of insects haunting the arctic region. Herewith, the bloodsucking mosquitos and black flies are on top of the list, badgering mooses and reindeer, driving them to desparation.

The pier in Kebnats fills with backpacks and people, who were sitting with us in the bus minutes ago or who came here by their own cars or just returned from a daytour in the surrounding mountains. But all want to cross the lake and stay at least one night in the STF-station on the other side.

The fjällstation Saltoluokta is one of the first huts for wanderers that was raised by the STF (Svenska Turistföreningen) more than 100 years ago and is simultaneously the one with the richest tradition. Many tours into the fjäll (i.e. the mountains) may start here, either following the King's Path (Kungsleden) or into the nationalparks Stora Sjöfallet, Muddus and Sarek. The Sarek is our aim. Saltoluokta is one of the few accesses into this special nationalpark.

The Sarek-Nationalpark in the Swedish part of Lapland is a mountainscape coming up with peaks over 2.000 m height, which is unusual for all the other mountains being polished by ice-age glaciers. The Sarek forms together with the nationalparks and natural reserves Muddus, Stubba, Sjaunja, Stora Sjöfallet, Padjelanta and Tjuolda the UNESCO-World Cultural Heritage „**Laponia**".

The Sarek still belongs to the reindeer farming area of the Sami. The paths used by the laplanders for this purpose naturally lead through easily accessible valleys in this alpine region. The classic ways go through Njoatosvágge, Guhkesvágge, Ruohtesvágge and Guohpervágge. Due to its difficult accessibility by wide birch tree forests Rapadalen is unsuitable thereto.

In 1909, the Sarek was declared to a nationalpark at the instigation of the Swedish geographer Axel Hamberg (1863 – 1933). Axel Hamberg explored this park methodically within nearly 40 years and thank to his efforts the untouched nature was preserved from being exploited by the wheelings and dealings of the hydropower companies.

In contrast to other nationalparks and reserves there are neither shelters nor marked ways for minimizing the number of visitors simply by non-offering any kind of convenience. There are only a few bridges over rivers, which were built primarily for the interests of the Sami. Temporarily trails, existing for decades, were erased from the region map BD10 of the Nya Fjällkartan series.

The landscape is rich in variety and offers deeply indented dells, mountains and glaciers as well as one or another plateau. In addition to that – at the southern edge of the nationalpark, but yet beyond its border – one will find the sensational natural spectacle the river Rapa (i.e. Rapaätno, with ätno = river) has shaped in eons – its picturesque delta before the Rapa enters the lake Laitaure. It is an unforgettable view from the unsecured edge of the 700 m precipitous south flank of the mountain Skierffe on the delta and the ice-aged born trough valley Rapadalen.

The STF-Station Saltoluokta is run by a team of young people – mostly students. Young lads or girls can apply to the STF for such a job meeting people from overall the world during the semester break in one of the managed cabins.

The young people are completely down-to-earth. As I was in preparations for our adventurous journey I mailed my request for depositing two postal packages in the station on beforehand. That were no issue, I was told and thus, I sent two banana boxes by snail-mail to Saltoluokta jam-packed with food and spirit (which is not allowed in aeroplanes as well as gas).

Julia, who was my email counterpart during the preparation period and whom I am glad to meet face-to-face today, leads Niklas and me down into the basement and hands the two banana boxes over to us.

Outside the station is a wooden platform directly next to the main building. We spread ourselves majestically out. It is a hell of a lot of stuff in these two boxes. Well, nearly 40 kg food and methylated spirit occupy much space.

We actually need 3 hours for portioning out, packing and tidying up the platform. Most of the heavy stuff is packed on Jens's carriage. But it is always the same thing: the setting sights on the individual maximum weights are exceeded this time again. I had hoped to get out of this job with a burden between 30 (haha) and 35 kg. And for Niklas I expected a maximum limit of 25 kg. Now his backpack weighs impressive 32 kg and mine is about 38 kg. We couldn't put Jens's sledge on the hook of the spring scale, hanging under the ceiling of the verandah near the main entrance of the old, tradition-rich building. I am absolutely sure here we are dealing with something around the 40-kg-mark, too.

At this point there is some need to waste a few words about the planned route. I thought a long time about a nice route with the map BD10 nailed onto the wall, covering the distances with a mileometer and eyeballing critically contour lines being suspiciously at close quarters. The result was a route of about 130 km, starting in Saltoluokta and ending in Kvikkjokk. At the beginning a motorboat should bring us across the lake Sitojaure and lateron the first section would take us from its western shore through the narrow Basstavágge, afterwards passing one of the most beautiful glacial lakes in the Sarek, the Bierikjavrre, then up to Mikkastugan in the heart of the park. Next through the Alggavágge almost till its end in the west, but then turning to the south through Niejdariehpvágge, crossing Sarvesvágge and ascent to the plateau Luohttoláhko. It should grow narrow from this point, namely again to the north, down from 1300m to a bit more than 800 m through Noajdevágge; a hairpin bend to the right heading to south again through Lullihavágge till the foot of the mountain massiv Skájdetjahkka. The next 4 to 5 days should see us on 3 daytrips into the surrounding area, before Boarektjahkka would be circumnavigated partially followed by passing the Sami settlement Boarek for finally reaching the Kungsleden. This one we wanted to follow for the last kilometers till Kvikkjokk, and hopping on a bus there, which would take us back to Gällivare (*see map on page 10*).

However, it was not to be. What actually happened, the gracious reader will learn by the description of the second day's march.

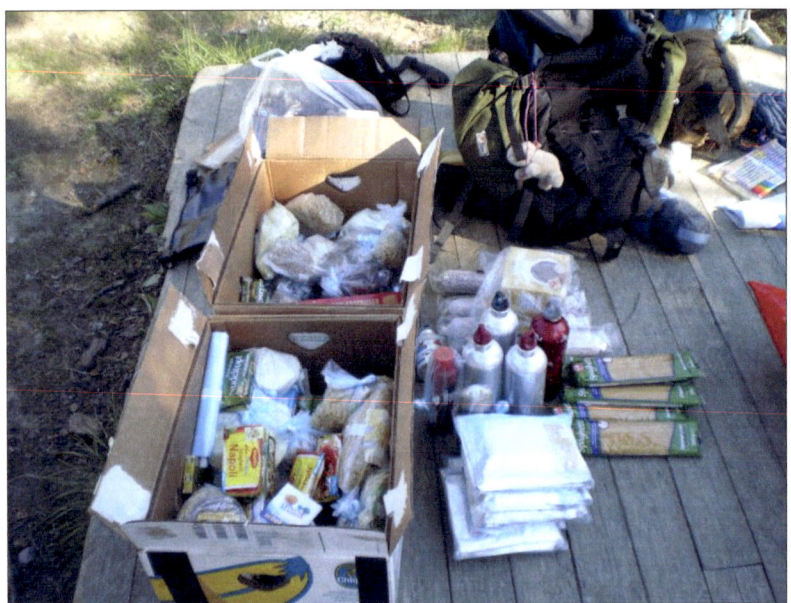

CARE Packets sent ahead

...just till over there!

Day 1 | July, 16th:
From Saltoluokta up to the Treeline

The weather is bombastically fine. Ready at last. After weeks of planning and a number of years of deprivation I am simmering with excitement the first steps as I did the first time. I am back again. Seems, that nothing has changed. I close my eyes, breathe deeply. The clear northland air let me fall into euphoria. The smell of the long-serving equipment, which cannot be washed away awakes memories and expectations simultaneously. Hamsun could have described it as follows: *I am muzzy of blessedness.*

Those, who weren't lucky enough yet to experience nature that way, can hardly be able to relate to actually looking forward to a debilitating time of privation.

The journey begins! The first stage leads us through coniferous forest with strong, old trees. The path is well-worn in the proximity of the tourist station. This first hop starts immediately over 430 m meters high – on an arduous distance about just 4 km. Being on a very low level – almost 400 m over sea level – lovely weather sends up the temperature to higher regions. That brings the most bloodthirsty monster of the northern hemisphere into the arena: the mosquito.

> *In the evening, a little before the sun went down, I was assailed by such multitudes of gnats as surpass all imagination. They seemed to occupy the whole atmosphere, especially when I travelled through low or damp meadows. They filled my mouth, nose and eyes, for they took no pains to get out of my way. Luckily they did not attack me with their bites or stings, though they almost choked me. When I grasped at the cloud before me, my hands were filled with myriads of these insects, all crushed to pieces with a touch, and by far too minute for description. The inhabitants call them Knort or Knott.*
>
> [Linné2, pg. 115f]

Due to Niklas's school holidays we had to swallow the bitter pill to travel in the summertime, the heyday of the mosquito plague.

Only 100 m onwards I must declare: I am struggling. My muscles are totally played out. It was no good idea not to do any sports for months. One cannot compensate that with a handful of test runs with duration of 1 or 2 hours, fully laden with sandbags in the backpack. The result can be seen here and now. Every 50 meters I must pause for breath. And what about the son?

Niklas gets on well with his baggage despite the strikingly increased weight on his back than planned. But nevertheless I am sure to read great fascination for the unique landscape in his face. He has no problems to keep in step with Jens, the old mountain goat, who is the fittest of us, anyway. The two of them produce a distance to me that I cannot really decrease until the last days of our journey.

After all, the cloudless sky makes for bright blue lakes surrounded by the fresh green of birch trees and coniferous forest. The view from our elevated position – beyond the treeline now - on the lakes Langas and Pietsaure and the mountains around them are absolutely stunning.

We raise the tent at a small streamlet. Hooray! I am a total wreck – and thus after only a few hours. My energy will be just enough for not more than a quick wash. I wonder what all this will come to. I hope that it will be as in the last tours and usually only the first one or two days will be horrible and torturous for neck and shoulder regions. But who knows - possibly I am just too old for this shit.

It has cooled down significantly since the morning hours. There are only 7° or 8° C left (*i.e. 44-46° F*) regarding the 20° through the rest of the day. Despite the fact, that it is still as bright as day. Thus, it is not correct to speak of night chills. Of course, the sun will approach the horizon more and more during the day, depending on how far in the north one is and depending on how far advanced the period of the midnight sun actually is, the sun vanishes behind it or not.

This first day was a thrilling experience for Niklas. Even though it started with mosquito attacks. The good news is, that we could buy a locally well-known mosquito spray and stick in the shop of the station. On the other hand the drop-dead gorgeous blue sky and the view back on the lakes and the mountains around them could compensate all negativities.

Niklas's burned foot didn't make any problems – everything is fine. Even my knee, which participated in a meniscus surgery in the last days of March, kept quiet. There were absolutely no troubles – despite of the heavy backpack and the persistent northgoing. Hope, it will not change in the next 3 weeks.

Today's supper is composed of salami, crispbread, cereal bar and tea.

...just till over there!

Afterwards all members of the expedition bring theirselves as one man without any delay to a horizontal position. After all the first stage combined with the bus ride was exhausting enough.

View from the Main Building in Saltoluokta

Looking back to the Lake Langas

Day	distance km	meters up + down	start Level	end Level	peaks, rivers, lakes on the way
1	4	325	375	700	Junction for Pietsaure Ahutjkarsa (600 m) Autsutj-jakka Lulep Kierkau (1139 m)
Cumulated Values	4	325			

...just till over there!

Day 2 | July, 17th:
Treeline till short before Sitojaure

The new day begins as the previous one ended: it's all guns and roses. But we can hardly speak about a „new" day as the last one actually didn't end. Thanks to the midnight sun it is as bright as day twentyfour-seven.

This pleasant atmosphere and a soft breeze that keeps the mosquitos at distance suggest it being a good idea to take breakfast under the open sky. We cosy up on the juniper trees, which spread across the whole area, rolling in the compulsary muesli for warming up and finally nibbling at some pieces of

> *The Laplanders are perhaps so called from the (Swedish) word lappa, to sew or patch together, because their garments usually answer to that description.*
> *[Linné2, pg. 130]*

crispbread with honey on it. Leisurely – so we are away on vacation - we enjoy the situation before easygoing packing of the backpacks starts.

Meanwhile one or two clouds still appear and thus, we start with sunny, only partially cloudy sky. After the 4 km we made yesterday, there are about 16 km till Sitojaure still ahead. There is a mobile phone network still available and therefore I ring Erik-Ivar Kallok, one of the two Sami living at the lake Sitojaure, offering the service of boattransfers over the lake to Rinim, which is situated at the northwestern corner of the lake.

The connection is up and we signalize our arrival for the early „evening". At most of the greater lakes, Sami people regularly provide motorboat transfers across during the season. Outside the season in advanced autumn or autumn/winter, when the lakes are not yet frozen, wanderers **must** cross a lake by rowing (as far as the STF holds rowing boats available here). Otherwise one can be out of luck suddenly being forced to bypass a great natural obstacle. Thus, the Sami developed additional sources of income. It is a fact that only a few Sami can exist by breeding reindeer as the only source of revenue.

The Sami are the aboriginal people in Lapland. Nowadays, they inhabit the northern and central part of the Scandinavian Peninsula. They were and still are often referred to as "Laps" or "Laplanders". The origin of the expression „Lap", which had always been like that, traces back to the physical appearance of representatives from this ethnicity and actually is obscure. According to age and origin of different sources, the terms are „Laps", „Sami", Sapmi" or even „Laplanders". The Sami call themselves "Sameh", which means as much as swamp people. What all of these sources unanimously underline is the condescension and viciousness of the expression "Lap" for their people. Some interpretations of this expression believe this feeling being dependent on inflection and intonation of the term. Finally, the origin of the expression „Lap" is not clarified undoubtedly.

Depending on the dominating living space one differentiate between Mountain Laps, Lake Laps, who preferably live from fishing in Norway and the Wood Laps. Furtheron, there is the group of Finnmark Laps in Northern Norway and the group of Skolt Laps, who settle in the environment of the Finnish lake Inari and in Russia. Nowadays, the number of all Sami in Finland, Norway, Sweden and Russia decreased down to circa 70.000.

Originally, the Sami were nomads nothing more than hunters and gatherers. The reindeer husbandry and breeding is not as old as one might think. The oldest evidences for this are from about 800 Anno Domini and as from about 1500 Anno Domini there were nearly no wild reindeer left. Today, only 10% of all Sami can subsist on reindeer breeding and fishing alone. Nevertheless, reindeer husbandry is an important profession, considerably more a lifesyle and hence a very important part of the Sami identity.

The Sami practice a shamanic religion. In their opinion nature is living and inspired and thus, they offer sacrifices to e.g. stones, rocks and lakes at so-called *Seitas* as they call their sacrificial altars. The magic drum and the „*Joiken*" (Sami chanting) are a centrality in the Sami shamanism. During religious ceremonies the shaman consults

Such as live in the forests are dexterous marksmen, but not those who inhabit the alps. Nevertheless, they all contrive, by means of their wooden bows, to procure, in the course of the winter, a considerable number of squirrels (...) for the sake of their skins. [Linné2, pg. 49]

The inhabitants of this country no longer use bows and arrows, but rifle-guns loaded with bullets, not with small shot. [Linné1, pg. 137]

the magic drum and joiks until walking on air. By doing this he can see into the netherworld and the future.

In *joiking,* the Sami sing the praise of men, animals and natural phenomenons. One does not joik *about* something, but joiks a person, a mountain, a river, a nice place and thus expresses his feelings for this being or natural beings. This kind of music will not be composed – it is simply existing. Joiking is something from the pre-christian era of the Sami, it is part of life. On the other hand, the joik can only partly be characterized as improvisatory chanting – it simply exists and adapts itself to the atmosphere and the landscape.

The garb of the Sami is an important symbol for their identity and affiliation. Form and color disclose the region the bearer comes from. The radiant colors of the cloth (green, blue, red and yellow) are remarkable. These colors, the „national colors", find themselves in the flag of Sapmi, which was established in 1992. The colors symbolize different elements in the Sami life. **Green** stands for the nature and plants, which make for surviving. **Blue** stands for water that is essential for all living things. **Red** stands for fire that gives off heat and is the symbol for love. **Yellow** is the sun, which stands for longevity. The circle symbolizes the magic drum.

Flag of Sapmi

*

The catastrophe overtakes us after walking for only 2 km. Jens – who was streets ahead of us as usual – suddenly veers to the right. Looking like a dying duck in the thunderstorm, when Niklas and I approach, he tells us, that the "trolley experiment" failed. One of the two shafts of the trolley that are made from aluminium pipes is nearly completely broken. The fact is that we cannot continue using the apparatus furtheron.

Now there is need to revise the current plan and choose a new route. Jens wants to re-import his vehicle into Switzerland and that means that we cannot end our tour in Kvikkjokk, but are forced to return to Saltoluokta by passing the place we are now and catching the apparatus.

We deposit the trolley about 50 m out of the way at a small water course, but in direct line to a hut mentioned in the map and being in the environment of the river Avtsusjjåhkå. We memorize this place well - in real life as well as in the map – since we want to retrieve and garn the apparatus 3 weeks later.

Henceforth, Jens is walking in „vintage style", i.e. with the backpack actually on his back. The path drags on forever and a day. I realize my powers fading. Even after a break of a full hour things are over and done, so what concerns my person.

It's a different thing regarding Niklas – the guy is all there. Well, in the bloom of youth your power seems never ending. Kudos! The truth is, at the moment I am the weakest team member. But there is no reason for depressions figuring contemporaries from my circle of friends and acquaintances being in my current situation, while I'm creaking out of my sitting position – and promptly I'm feeling back on top again. Sometimes such a psycho-shit for motivation rules!

In the meanwhile we have reached the edge of the high plain, which allows us a first view on the Sitojaure. And hence we reached a point, where we are forced to carry on walking, because there is no running water (for drinking and cooking) close by. We are in close vicinity to the mountain Tjirák (1003 m). From this place it's going downhill – into the birch tree forest. We will not make it till the lake today.

Niklas is tuckered out, as I myself. I am not able to walk 50 m at a stretch. Then I need a breather. Another few meters: breather! Feet, shoulders, rump, leg biceps - I'm totally exhausted.

There are only 2 km left till Sitojaurestugorna, when we cross a creek. With a small piece of ground to raise the tent – amidst the forest. That's a rarity. We will stay here. Shortly after coming to a stop, a cloud of mosquitos cocoons us. Despite all physical deficiencies we suffer from at this moment, the tent raises within record time, all important equipment and at the end ourselves launched into it. The tent entries will be sealed and now we can sigh with relief. But one thing has to be done before peace will come: the ritual mosquito slaughter. Fleabags! Rabble! Only a dead mosquito is a good mosquito.

It's a pity: the buzzing suckers always win out. The only way open to us is to cook inside the tent. Otherwise the bloodthirsty beasts would suck us dry. No one can move normally in the tightness of our mobile home.

Silently vegetating, I am hardly able to move any part of my body. After two marvelous trekking tours together with Jens in this scenery, there is confident hope, that he will continue traditional manners by taking control over the ladle. Furthermore I know for sure that his hunger limit is well below mine. For demonstrating good will, I pick one of the meths bottles from my backpack while lying on my back. I hand it over to him and drop back physically total down, miming the Dying Swan. Niklas doesn't move either – he seems to be gone into a short-term fixed coma.

Reliable going like a Swiss watch the Swiss confederate unwinds the cooking thing and at least proffers us a dumb noodle soup taken from the rich dry food fund. Along with it we have unchopped salami with residual crisp bread. Well, this will give us a leg-up! However, the opulent bar of chocolate should not be kept secret.

In a minute's silence we wonder about the murmur of a highway in the background. Highway? Here? Of course, not! It's the buzzing of clouds of mosquitos. I remember well the tour on the „Border path of Troms", which I walked with Oliver up to the Treriksröset (the border stone of three countries: Norway, Sweden and Finland), far further north. We had a nice camping ground at a nearby river, the Anjavasselva. In bright sunshine the mosquito bodies pelted like raindrops on the taut tent skin. Just, as if they had sounded the attack and tried to penetrate the outer skin like kamikaze pilots.

Due to the efforts of food intake entirely enfeebled, everyone lies around digesting more or less silently to oneself.

The trouble is, if you need going for a pee. Now is the time to open the tent – quickly crawling outside – and close the tent. While passing water take care of the buzzing breed for avoiding stings in the tallywacker.

What a shit, if precisely that is due: naked legs and more – an invitation to a banquet. So much hands for defending oneself nobody has. Thus, every defecation visualizes emphatically the helplessness of man against the forces of nature and rewards us regularly with a considerable number of stings so that we will remember it forever. Possibly even we are not that helpless and can play some tricks in this affair (*see tips: "Mosquitos" in the appendix*).

After having finished the business, it is advised to re-enter the tent as fast as possible. Entrance opened up – tired body in – entrance closed. With this occasion – and the previous one – illegally intruded mosquitos needed to be eliminated without any mercy for the purpose of peace at night (*see tips: mosquitos*). Hope, nobody is forced to leave the tent before morning.

The brightness of the „night" is a special experience. If you have never been lucky to experience it firsthand, you really cannot imagine the phenomenon of the midnight sun. Many a person has trouble dealing with the problem to fall asleep under a blazing fly. Sometimes I make a blindfold from a scarf for easier falling asleep. Not so today. I am actually deadly exhausted. Let's see, what the next day will put forward.

...just till over there!

View on Sitojaure before us and Lake Langas behind us

Day	distance km	meters up + down	start Level	end Level	peaks/rivers/lakes on the way
2	14	150	700	630	Maskostjakka (1420 m) Sjaksjo (1250 m) Autsutj-jakka Tjirak (979 m)
Cumulated Values	18	475			

...just till over there!

Day 3 | July, 18th:

Sitojaure till Rengärde before Aktse

What a nice morning! It is sunny and partly clouded. Myriads of mosquitos are ever-present. Predecessors built a fireplace in form of the usual stone circle, where we stay. We make a fire in hopes of repulsing the mosquitos with the smoke. With a miserable result. After the morning routine we tidy up the campground and betake ourselves.

Yesterday we did more as assumed. Only a quarter later we reach the lakeshore. And we are in luck: there are 2 rowing boats on our side of the lake. That means we need to make the rowing tour across the Sitojaure about 4 km only once. We will recognize later, that the course is bouyed out with well-camouflaged black or other darkcolored plastic cans.

Here as well as at other lakes that are „crossed" by a trekking path looked after by the STF, rowing boats lay ready for use. All in all 3 of them with at least one must be available on each side. That's the rule everyone, who wants to use the boats, must obey. From this it follows immediately, that the wanderer reaching the lake and finding only one boat on the bank is forced to cross the lake three times: the first time with the discovered boat, the second time back with another boat in tow and the

> I here obtained a curious piece of information respecting the mode of castrating the reindeer. When the animal is two years and a half old, its owner (...) getting a person to assist him by holding it fast by the horns, places himself betwixt its hind legs. He then applies his teeth to the scrotum, so as to bruise its contents, but not so as to break the skin, for in that case the reindeer would die. He afterwards bruises the part still more effectually between his fingers. The same operation is performed on both sides, if the reindeer remains quiet long enough for the purpose at one time. (...) This is certainly an art, no less curious than remarkable, (...).   [Linné2, pg. 3]

third time with only one boat again. Sometimes you are in luck and there is a guy on the opposite bank, who wants to go in the opposite direction at the very moment you arrive there. In this case you would have saved two debilitating exercises.

Loading the boat is more than trivial because of the high total weight we offer. It has to be pushed somewhat into the water firstly. Then the main part of all the heavy luggage can be heaved over the ship's side. It is no wonder that sharp stones and wet logs serving as a landing pier are highly slippery and it is a great challenge to balance on them. Well, with some efforts we make it and now we are going to speed up the container vessel – with a load capacity of about 330 kg.

The technical state of the suspension of the boat oars is beneath contempt. The oars are fixed somehow with rope ends to short planks being mounted perpendicularly to the rail and in addition to that are unequally long and loose. Ducting the oars properly is nearly impossible and thus the first meters take a disagreeable course.

Fixing of the Oars

„Let's try to row with two of us simultaneously: one on the left side, the other one on the right side", Niklas proposes.

Okay, this plan will be put into action by Jens and Niklas. Due to the uneven length of the oars extending into the water and the lousiest way of fixing them, the attempt has to be regarded as failed after a few minutes.

„We are going to paddle", I say. "Just like sitting in a dragonboat! There are three oars onboard, so everyone can join the party!"

But this method isn't a scream, either. To be honest, it works even worse than the galley variant.

„OK, I will do it alone. But you need to spell me", Jens says. This practice turns out to be the best one. Sometimes I step in steering the course with the superfluous third oar, while sitting on the podestal like stern.

...just till over there!

As mentioned before we suffer from slightly optical-sensorical problems to recognize the (dark colored) moored buoys on the (dark) water. No wonder we are sauntering promptly in the complete wrong direction. It takes only a very short time, when a loud shout coming from the lakeside makes us aware of this. Someone living in the hereabouts established Sami settlement gets us back on the straight and narrow. We continue wobbling with the insufficient tools over the complete distance of 4 km – and finally we reach the opposite lakeside, where it started to rain just in the moment we are on sure ground again.

We enter a so-called Vindskydd, which is a spartanly equipped small mountain hut, and have a tea break. In the meanwhile defining to make the way back deviating from the former planning across the Sitojaure again, we want to deposit a little of our burden here and regain it then. Thus, we leave some food (amongst it a whole salami) and the now useless tools for Jens's trolley properly packed and hidden for prying eyes under the jacked up hut at its backside.

We exercise patience as the rain grows stronger. At last it slackened and we are looking forward to continue the walk in rain jackets. But in the end the rain stops and the rain clothing can stay in the backpacks. The only protection we install are wrappers for the backpacks, if further showers should follow.

The path sucks. Stone after stone criss-crossing everywhere and planks over long distances, partly overgrown with birch trees and willows. Time and again they are nearly pushing the wanderer away from the planks, which is sometimes up to 1 m above boulder sections.

Here again the mosquitos are in high number. Each time pausing for taking breath, one is immediately covered by clouds of these damned bloodsuckers. Oh horror!

What follows are 100 very steep meters in height, hardly missing the 939 m peak height of the Martevárásj at it's right side, up onto the 4 km wide high plain situated just before the lake Laitaure. On the left hand, a little beyond the path, we see a reindeer corral, which is marked as a circular symbol on the map and described with "rengärde". I remember it being already here when I was here together with Oliver some 30 years ago. And it seems that it still in usage by the Laps probably for branding or neutering the creatures.

Below the corral a watercourse is drawn on the map, which is the only source of water in the proximity. I am rather exhausted and glad that we have chosen this camp ground.

Alas, the watercourse is dry and there is no other flowing surface water on the whole plain. There are 3 tiny puddles instead, glittering in the sunlight, but without any in- or outlet. Ponding water. After all it is not brackish and superficially clear. It will be sufficient for washing off the sweat. And a tea with boiled water for killing the germs will not kill us.

The tent is up within a few minutes. A bathing session before having dinner will do the best for perking up. One of the puddles willingly receives our sweaty naked bodies not without stirring up the sandy ground as we plunge into the water.

I guess that this kind of bathing in the wild is absolutely to his liking by looking at my son. Obviously he gets a kick out of it. He as well as Jens and I enjoys the feeling of freedom by doing it.

The wide plain is sun-drenched. Sometimes cumulus clouds establish in the sky. They are of moderate mightiness, what implies that it probably will stay dry. The air is clear and we had an incredible wide view.

In direction of march the lake Laitaure with the station Aktse at its waterside hides away in the next valley, but the mountains behind are clear in sight. Pure nature – nothing else! No streets, houses, power poles or something similar. And no soul in sight to disturb the peace

They always construct their huts in places where they have ready access to clear cold springs.
[Linné1, pg. 126,]

We allow ourselves fried potatoes with salami and enjoy this flamboyant meal under the open sky.

A light breeze keeps the mosquitos at distance. There has been no rain since we left the vindskydd.

Day	distance km	meters up + down	start Level	end Level	peaks, rivers, lakes on the way
3	6	310	630	940	Sitojaurestugorna Fjällstation Kablajaure (rowing 4 km) Vindskydd Kablajaure Martevaratj (939 m) Rengärde Place-of-3-Puddles
Cumulated Values	24	785			

...just till over there!

Puddles in the High Plain

Raising Tent below Reindeer Fence

...just till over there!

Day 4 | July, 19th:
Rengärde till Place-of-2-Bridges

It is nippy out there, i.e. outside the sleeping bag. There is no necessity to rise before waking up. Or was it vice versa? Never mind, in any case nobody feels the urge to leave the kip bag, which was aerated continuously with warm air. And suddenly you are caught between Scylla and Charybdis, triggered by morning bladder pressure. The only options are either to let it run warm and wet (this only a theoretical option) or to bring oneself to get up – leave the tent – and return into the bag. If you see a man about a horse, it needs to be.

Breakfast must be had inside the tent this morning – due to the mosquitos. Do they never sleep?

Today, I'm well on track – there is no comparison to the first days. Those were sheer torture, especially regarding the latest ascent onto the high plain.

We are going to reach Aktse today, row across the lake Laitaure and continue the walk on the opposite bank for another few kilometers. There the further route runs for about 8 km through forest without leaving the 540 m contour line. Afterwards, back again above the treeline, additional 4 km will separate us from the vindskydd Rittak (on a height of circa 820 m). And another kilometer furtheron there is a (summer)bridge over the Jåkkejågásj, a water course coming directly from the high plain Ijvvárláhko – which is already in Sarek - flowing into the lake Tjaktjajaure. Thereupon – and especially onto its western end – one has an amazing view from an elevated position shortly before reaching Rittak and being simultaneously above the treeline. Reaching the bridge over the Jåkkejågásj, we will leave Kungsleden and proceed to the Sarek. This is the outlook on the next coming days.

But we are still on the high plain before Aktse, when a young man in shorts overtakes us striding assertively and greeting friendly. We should meet him again.

The unobstructed view to the wide landscape is impressive and uplifting. Ahead, i.e. pointing at 01:00, the mountain Tjahkelij pushes its 1200 m into the heavens. In the valley before, still out of sight, lies the lake Laitaure, revealing more and more of itself the closer we get to the steep descent to Aktse. Simultaneously with descending the Skierffe, Aktse's „own" mountain, appears in our vision range. With a 700 m vertically slopy rock face, Skierffe guards the picturesque river delta of Rapaätno,

...just till over there!

the river Rapa, created in eons. Deviating perpendicularly from Kungs-leden a path leads over 6 km to the top of Skierffe, which can be climbed easily from its backside, from where you can enjoy this unique spectacle of nature. Doing this, one can leave his name in a guestbook on the peak. It is put into a metal box at the foot of a significant stone mark.

We reach the junction for the Skierffe, but due to the adverse weather conditions decide against this detour, which would cost us a whole day in the end. From the junction the descent starts directly and steep and leads over strenuous 300 meters in height through thick forest down. As we are sinking deeper continuously (back to circa 450 m above mean sea) – at perceived tropical temperatures – the number of active bloodsuckers increases exponentially with every meter further downhill. The mosquito nets were no false purchase! But nevertheless we rake umpteen mosquito bites in. *Pox, pestilence and cholera are not more than a snailshit compared to the true scourge for mankind: the mosquito!*

A lightly loaded gal overtakes us swiftly. An elder Swede pauses by a water course, which actually is the central water supply for Aktse down in the valley. The path stretches like chewing gum. One sees the first of the cabins, when getting his nose flattened at its wooden wall. Jens, the old mountain goat, has already reached the station and talks to the young wanderer, who overtook us on the high plain. Niklas and I are going to join them.

„Hej, my name is Hans", he says.
„Fine", I say, „than we can speak German."
„Oh, I'm Swedish. I don't understand you", he rejoins.

He pretends to be Swedish with his height of 175 to 180 cm, raven-haired and dark-complexioned as it is usual on the Indian subcontinent. Along with it brown eyes and pearl white teeth ad nauseam. Of course, the typical Swede straight from the book.

He is a real sunnyboy and consistently likeable. We learn, that he wants to do the complete Kungsleden – from Abisko to Ammarnäs -, which means about 450 km. He will decide in Kvikkjokk, a small village that he will reach in probably 3 days, whether to continue his journey or not. Kvikkjokk means half the distance. At the moment he is in doubt, whether to go beyond Kvikkjokk. We will see.

Now Hans is to cross the Laitaure – and we as well. Jens already arranged to do it together with him, i.e. all four of us rowing the same boat. Thus, we can share out the work of rowing over 3 km between us.

...just till over there!

Aktse is one of the few fjäll stations, which can proudly present a provisions store and so, Jens proposes to buy canned Köttbullar (meat balls) destroy the two tin cans for supper – together with mashed potatoes. Who on earth can say no to this?

We drink a little water before walking the next kilometer almost exclusively along the typical wood nailer path to the landing stage. And we are in luck again: two boats waiting for us gently bobbing up and down. Hurray – only rowing once the distance! We pack up everything and have a keen eye on getting a little water below the keel from the start before the complete luggage is inside the boat. The gross tonnage (4 people plus backpacks) is about 390 kg. Accordingly the dinghy lies low in the water and in connection with the current light waves it reacts very slowly to our efforts to cope with the defective sweeps. Changing places, when the rowing part is to be done by someone else, is a rare fun. It is a truly tender subject.

Skipper Jens rowing

The solitary wanderer standing on the landing stage at the opposite lakeside sees the dinghy lurching about, but doesn't care about it. The German claims not to be a world rowing champion, either and only hopes to reach the other side. Hans tends to relax in the refuge on this lakeside before continuing his march. But we like to walk on immediately and say goodbye not without the promise to send him copies of the pictures I made of him in the boat after our return home. He is really pleased with that as he actually doesn't have any photographical documentation about his expedition.

*

Well, we start again. Halfway between our current position at the Laitaure and the vindskydd Rittak are two bridges in the middle of the forest and only 200-300 m apart. One of them traverses the mountain torrent Suobbatjåkkå and the other – as seen from our perspective the first one – a small offset of the same. This is the aim for today's stage. Thus, there are cool 4 km before us.

After an hour's march through thick coniferous forest I feel definitely my sinking strength and feel relieved when we reach the first bridge.

It is a place of perfect idyll. Two creeks come together in a pond like widening, for flowing in a shared riverbed afterwards. Conifers all around, some birch trees strayed in between. The stony soil is mostly overgrown. Shortly: a little paradise – neglecting the mosquitos!

We have the possibility to raise the tent on a relative woodless earth buckle. My weary legs find it absolutely first class here and are just propping up as my fellow campaigners decide to check the situation at the other bridge. Well, all right, let's go – but without the backpacks!

This place is totally different from the first one. Much more rugged, not that soft. The mountain torrent is a raging stream that rushes noisily beneath the wooden construction of the bridge. It is much more difficult to find a fine bathing place here. On the other hand there is an often used camp ground directly near the water, too. Jens and Niklas find a big

> *The weather became very close; the mosquitos aggregate in swarms and I was forced to smoke tobacco all the time for getting rid of them.* [Hamsun, pg. 930]

cooking pot, which they confiscate immediately for our huge portion of Köttbullar awaiting us this evening.

Well, in the end we choose the idyll. On the way back to there we meet Hans again. He looks tired as well, but will go on till Rittak, where he wants to make a break.

After raising the tent we take a bath in the picturesque, pond like leachings, created by the two creeks flowing together. The water is damned cold – colder than expected in this idyllic environment – but refreshing.

The available fireplace serves for preparing the dinner – mainly for generating smoke to keep the mosquitos at distance. Alas, it only works semi-well. Niklas quarrels with the mosquito plague for the first time and feels personally followed by them.

Smokey Fire against the Flying Enemy

He tries a new creative way to manage the overwhelming mass of flying buzzers. The soil is refreshing thick here, not the way as in the higher fjäll. Thus, he is striding to the water course and lays a mask of mud on hair and arms.

Looks a bit ridiculous, but actually works. The disadvantage of this solution is the inevitable filth in removing the stuff. One should do it before entering the sleeping bag. Due to that procedure, there was no repetition in trying this again.

The meal was excellent and abundant. Köttbullar till the cow comes home. Before having tea I feel a digestive urge to swivel sideways into the bushes. I quickly find an odd-shaped rock predestinated as a thunder-box. There are actually excellent conditions, if there weren't those trunk bearing beasts. Hardly that the pants slip down the thighs turn black. You cannot concentrate on your core business and despite all efforts to chase the mosquitos a considerable number of bites will be added to the already existing ones. All right, that is just the way things are.

If you are not in a hurry you may use prophylactics in repelling the aggressors concerning exposed body parts. (*see tips: mosquitos*).

At teatime we clear off into the lounge. In the meanwhile, Niklas has a desilting and Jens is going to share his lament.

...just till over there!

Niklas's Muddy Mask

„Rats! Being here at one of most beautiful places you can imagine and you cannot enjoy it because we are forced to hole up due to these damned bloody critters!"

Imagine hearing this tirade in the glorious Saxon tongue. I agree apathetically and count just for fun the bites of the gnats only on my left foot. Mind you, 30 in these few first days. But what of it – if the level of itching is acceptable...

At dusk the sun arises between the clouds. I take the opportunity to make a photographic excursion. Without any haste, free from hurrying, I enjoy the silence of the evening wilderness. The roaring water course beneath the next bridge is out of earshot – not a breeze carrying its voice across. The ludic water courses in our idyllic corner only bring off a soft purling of the stream. Now and then a little bird beeps somewhere in the trees –

The inhabitants of Westbothnia, to defend themselves against the bites of gnats, besmear their skin with a mixture of tar and fish-grease, or some other kind of fat. They keep this composition in a horn which hangs at their side. The Laplanders however give themselves no trouble about any such matter. *[Linné2, pg. 108]*

for the rest is completely silent. And beautiful. The air is clean and pure and „smells" good. Different from ours in the „Pott" (*the Ruhr area in Germany; remark by the author*), even if the smokestacks of the coal mines actually do not dominate the scene any longer. The evaporations of the megacity from Duisburg to Dortmund – quasi a continuous urban area – have a lasting effect on the climate there.

Picturesque Wooden Bridge

From our elevated camp ground the slopes of the Sarek mountains far in the west can be seen across the slender and high fir trees. The Kungsleden leads in front of them, which we will leave in northern direction tomorrow. Thus, we will enter directly the heights. A simple, old and slanting bridge lights in the foreground – the timber fade, nearly white. The clear water crossed by it houses clean flushed rocks.

Later, it starts to drizzle a bit. Temperatures are mild and it is a pleasure to move within this marvelous nature.

I am very satisfied with myself and the world.

Day	distance km	meters up + down	start Level	end Level	peaks, rivers, lakes on the way
4	10	490	940	540	Tareaive (1083 m) Junction for Skierffe Aktse Fjällstation Rapadelta Tjakkeli (1214 m) Nationalpark Border Place-of-2-Bridges
Cumulated Values	34	1275			

...just till over there!

Day 5 | July, 20th:
Place-of-2-Bridges till High Plain of Ijvvárlahko

It rains often in showers during the night. Drizzle. The sky is overcast in the morning. Though there are dark clouds above, there is no further rain. Seems I laid on a boss in the ground the whole night long – as a result my back suffers. But no matter.

We put our packages together and start again. Continuing up through

> The fire-places here were furnished with a regular apparatus for boiling the kettle. The Laplanders in general content themselves for this purpose with a large stick, which they place obliquely in the ground, so as to lean over the fire, and on which they suspend either a kettle or a fish (...)   [Linné1, pg. 198]

wood and mosquitos. Partly young birch trees grow close to the beaten track resp. to the boardwalks, trying to cling to the backpacks with their branches. Fortunately, however, this is the case only for a short distance of a few hundred meters. Then it gets steadily upwards. Estimated 200 m difference in altitude, with a rather steep beginning.

Sooner as expected we reach the vindskydd Rittak. Since a short while we are walking on Sarek grounds. The Kungsleden cuts the most southeast corner of the Sarek nationalpark for a distance of about 15 km.

We make an extended break in Rittak. Jens finds some leftovers of provisions another wanderer has left here. Besides clearly identifiable muesli (marked with „morgenmat" on the plastic bag) there are some small bags with wheat like content and the Swedish workinstruction „tillsat 1 ¼ dl vand". We think it to be a baking mixture, which needs to be mixed with water and then baked, fried or whatever to be done with.

„Nothing ventured, nothing gained", Niklas murmured and starts kneading the dough. We fry the blanks in the Trangia-pot with the help of a little fat and thus, we've got some cookies – we call them *Vindskydd-Burgers* –, which do not taste bad.

The vindskydd is situated between the fjällstations Aktse and Pårte and divides the complete distance of 22 km in parts of 12 km (including a rowing part) and 10 km. By that means, the average distance between the single stations will level off at moderate 10 km. Though conceived as an emergency refuge, Rittak is regularly used as a stage finish.

Having crossed the narrow „thermal break" housing some arms full of firewood in one corner, the eyes are pleased by taut and sleek designed furniture of the only room inside. Beneath the single window opposite the door is a small desk. Two plank beds at the long side offer room enough for 4-6 sleepers – depending on how cosy the tired visitors want to be – and a rustic small iron stove completes the furnishings and fittings to the best use.

Vindskydd Interior

Weather increases steadily. The sky opens, the sun shines brightly. We continue our tour in direction to the bridge over the Jåkkejágásj. Till there we have to surmount a slight upgrade and reaching the bridge we will leave the path in the same moment and follow the watercourse coming from the north directly out of the Sarek. Another 200 meters in height up to the high plain Ijvvárlahko. Soft soil in combination with less stones pampers the feet.

Looking for a nice camp ground we walk a bit further over gently waved ground. Indeed, there are several nice places here amongst which we are free to choose. We select a beautiful location beneath a small hill, where we have left the backpacks before starting the detail search. A heavy breeze makes it difficult to raise the tent. Better not release the billowed out thing. On the other hand the wind keeps us free from mosquitos. The foot of the hill is a small stone field of midsize stones. Jens is going to build a kitchenette for our designer pots made of aluminium by means of rock panels as wind breaks. Thus, spaghetti with tomato sauce can be prepared without wasting too much fuel due to the strong wind. The noodles are delicious, but swallowed. In rounding out the menu we feed a final fatty broth.

Designer Kitchen „Laponia"

During the meal, Niklas proposes to make a daytrip to the top of the neighbour hill, the Favnoajvve tomorrow.

„Listen, it is early in the day. The weather is perfect. Why waiting till tomorrow?", Jens argued. Well, why not! And yes, he is really right with that. Well then, we start to go up from approximately 1000 to 1117 m.

On top it is even more windier, but we enjoy a bombastic view into the valley behind the mountain. We are standing just above the eastern end of the Tjaktjajaure and the following swamp area. Directly at our feet goes the Kungsleden – the part some 2 km behind the bridge, when we left it at midday today.

The wind blows fiercely. It is blowing us almost from our feet. We enjoy the majestic panorama in full. We can't get enough from the amazing view, but when we finally did, we moderately stroll back to the tent after we have inspected the rounded top of the hill.

We have a warm cup of tea as a nightcap before we vanish in the sleeping bags.

Bridge over the Jåkkejágásj

View from the Favnoajvve to South

Day	distance km	meters up + down	start Level	end Level	peaks, rivers, lakes on the way
5	14	460	540	1000	Partekietje (980 m) Vindskydd Rittak Huornatj (884 m) Favnoaivve (1117 m) Bridge over Kallekjakka Highplain Ijvvarlahko
Cumulated Values	48	1735			

...just till over there!

Day 6 | July, 21ˢᵗ:
High Plain of Ijvvárlahko till Bridge across Gådokjåhkå

There is a crackling sound on the tent's skin. Freezing rain! And it is cool. Reason enough for us to stay in the warmth for now. Not before afternoon we leave the camp ground, which is situated between Favnoajvve and Stuor Dágár. We want to approach more and more the Sarek and settle a base camp for daytrips anywhere. Therefore we selected one of the few bridges in Sarek as preferred location. This bridge spans an impressive gorge of the Gådokjåhkå, which is mainly fed from the glacier of the Bårdde Massif and diverse inflows from neighbouring valleys. It flows from West to East – partially through a narrow canyon – and runs into the Rapaätno.

The path is of good quality. Nice and soft soil. Then it will become corrugated. The ups and downs make me bad. But it's still okay.

It would be best to hike around the Stuor Dágár in the north direction along its west side and turn strictly left beneath the Suolanjunnje (1088 m) for walking then in direction NNW to the bridge.

The reason for doing that is simple: it is the wide swamp area Ijvvarláhko that should better be bypassed. The map legend calls it "bush vegetation" and it is highly recommended to avoid it.

„*Maior e longinquo reverentia* (observed from a distance, anything is beautiful). Thus quoth the Ancient Roman and that is exactly what we feel in view of the wide plain with – apparently – light bushes. No wonder that we are walking directly to the bridge, where we want to stay for some days, instead of making a detour round the bush vegetation.

But hardly entering these endless fields of willow bushes one sinks into that wet high moor up to the ankle. Walking through the belts of willows is debilitating. Now and then a small hill ascends out of the swamp, needs to be climbed up and back again, but at least the soil here is solid and comfortable to walk on.

After a break on top of one of those small hills we just are in the midst of another swamp section, when I hear an outcry accompanied by heaviest curses. I turn around and see Niklas hurling his backpack on the wet ground, roaming wild.

Why? His knife is gone. His selfmade knife he worked on for weeks, carving and smoothing down by the sweat of his brow. It is lost together with the hand tooled leather sheath. He fastened it with a short webbing to his belt, so that it was not situated directly under the waistbelt of the backpack and hanging a bit lower for not pinching on the hip bone. This webbing has become disconnected and knife including the sheath have been disbanded. Major desaster!

I walk over to him and try to lower the temperature. First we look around for the knife in immediate vicinity. Jens, who is already 200-300 m ahead notices, that something is wrong and returns without luggage back to us.

Niklas is beside himself.
„I do not go any further without my knife!" – Good grief!

At the last breakstone he still had it. He is sure about that. At least, that is an information on which we can build upon. Now, the only thing is to find that rock. The difficulty is to recognize it from the backside. We spread out and try to re-cover our tracks. If Niklas lost the darkbrown thing in the swamp inmidst the willow bushes, I am pessimistic about a positive result. Even on dry ground the probability to find a darkbrown, 20 cm long something on hardly covered soil is *1:manymanymany.*

I understand very well being emotionally charged, if one has given shape to an individual workpiece with astonishing attention to detail. Presumably it is the same with the Sami, when they manufacture their knives. Of course, there are products made by machines in the meanwhile, but on the other hand you may find many individual knife-makers, who partially are able to rely on their art to live. Traditionally Samis wear two knives in their belts – a big one and a small one, called stuorra niibi resp. unna nibas, what simply means big knife, small knife. Herewith, the small one has usually a blade between 12 and 18 cm, whereas the blade of the big one is between 18 and 25 cm. Of course there are differences. They are utility knives with strong blades and solid handles, used for fishing and hunting or carving.

Then the unimaginable happens: after one hour of intensive search we actually find the object of desire – about 200 m before re-entering the swampland. The jubilation knows no bounds!

But we are still not where we need to be. In the meantime we have passed the lakes 878, 879 and 874 being on the right-hand side. Swamp and heaps of earth alternate regularly with each other. Again, I am totally exhausted.

...just till over there!

Then, it appears ahead: the bridge. I hear my neck and shoulders rejoicing. Just a few hundred meters more. I'm sure, I will make it!

Finally we reach the bridge. A white impressive reindeer antler fixed on one of the bridge's pylons was visible from afar. Thus, we have had the aim in view for the whole last 500 m.

Before unpacking, we admire the river, being pressed through a narrow gorge nearby the bridge. A stupendous sight. Standing in the middle of the bridge, the raging and bubbling torrent, we can see through the metal walkway grid, calls for our utmost admiration for the forces of nature.

Today, we have walked for 6 hours and travelled a distance of about 12 km, mostly across difficult terrain. Tomorrow then will be a rest day.

Gådokjåhkå

Day	distance km	meters up + down	start Level	end Level	peaks, rivers, lakes on the way
6	10	100	1000	900	Stuor Takar (1162 m) Unna Jerta (983 m) Stuor Jerta (1335 m) Vaikautjakka (1307 m) Gadokjakkah
Cumulated Values	58	1835			

...just till over there!

Day 7 | July, 22nd:
Bridge across Gådokjåhkå | 1st Rest Day

What a wonderful morning. The tent stands only 10 m above the Gådokjåhkå, shortly before the river whooshes during the gorge, which is spanned by the bridge. The bridge itself is at 30 m distance from us. The water is pressed through the gorge and the roaring of the river does not stop, even during the night. On its further way to the Rapadalen the river finds its bed for a long stretch in a narrow canyon. Maybe we will see more of it on our exploratory walk to the Rapaätno.

There we will check, if a crossing of the wide Rapa is possible. If yes, we could continue our trek on the opposite=northern bank in direction to east and herewith to the fjällstation Aktse. Including an expensive boat transfer with Lennart, the Lap, right through the delta of the Rapa. In this case we wouldn't need to take the complete way there to our base camp indentically back to Saltoluokta.

A Rock in the Waves of the Gådokjåhkå

Today we have washing day, i.e. body wash. Niklas's experiences his ice water baptism – his first full-body ablution in the oh so ice cold glacial river. Compared to that the first bathing sessions were mere warm bathing days.

It is quite an effort for all of us, pouring the ice cold water in portions

...just till over there!

over arms and legs and even more for a full submersion. It takes your breath away for some seconds, when you are completely drowned in the water. But once being in it, it is simply marvelous. Nobody would stand it for a long time and might happen to do unskillfully steps back on land due to insensitive and numb feet from the ice water. Thus, it is recommended to wear any foot-protectors (sandals, old sport shoes or the like), for not getting hurt at sharp rocks. Having left the cool wet, one feels as if being newly born. Blood-circulation is in full swing, the wellbeing is indescribable. This cannot weaken the physical constitution and durability (*see Tip: Full-body Ablution*).

Bathing Spot on the Banks of the Gådokjåhkå Rapids

...just till over there!

Otherwise it is cool to enjoy and absorb the peace and serenity, which wilderness bestows. Between two lazy phases I'm out and about hunting for good photos in the near surroundings and capture some macro shots of mosses and lichens and skeletonized lemmings on celluloid.

And yes, I am accustomed to analog photography. With all means of film cartridges, manually adjusting the camera and film transport by thumb moves. Good, old Nikon F3, which is able to work on with 1/60 sec even in case of battery-exitus.

At some time or another we notice 2 wanderers crossing the bridge. It is a strategically point here, if you want to reach Sarvesvagge by walking through the valleys of the massif on the northern side of the river. In my opinion the bridge is nice to have but not indispensable for getting to the other bank. Only 200-300 m upstream the water level is low and the riverbed wide enough to cross it easily. Probably without changing the shoes. This merely underlines, that this bridge – as the others in Sarek – were not made for the concerns of wanderers but for the Sami. But who knows what it looks like at the time of the snow melt. Quite possible, that the water level is considerably increased then.

Not far from the bridge in a small cavern in the rocks of the gorge, three birch logs thick as a leg, each of them about one meter long force themselves into our consciousness. We kidnap them to the camp. A ransom demand does not appear to be appropriate as we cultivate thoughts to start a fire with them for roasting fine salami. In addition to the birch logs I find some faded and rotten remains of the old timber facing of the concrete bases of the bridge pylons. In the absence of other sources of wood in this treeless environment these were required without hesitation.

Without an axe we cannot get the birch logs small but they act as suppliers for ultra-thin birch tree bark, which is the best fire-starter ever. Some thin brush wood taken from near-earth juniper bushes serving for blasting the fire do the rest and soon, the flames within the ring of stones are blazing fiercely. The half of a salami – cut into slices and spitted – is a splendid appetizer. Okay, the edges get a bit carbonaceous sometimes, but we let us not let our cravings for something crunchy. Nitrosamine – pshaw! Blessed be, what feeds!

The then served pasta dish turns out to be bland. Spicing up with chili sauce peps up the whole thing and gives it a spicy aftertaste.

Thus, we finish the day having the traditional evening tea, accompanied by the continuing noise of the water.

...just till over there!

Moose Antlers

Another subject of inquiry is, why the Laplanders are so healthy; for which the following reasons may be assigned.

1. The extreme purity of the air, which seemed to give me new life as I inhaled it.
2. The use of food thoroughly dressed.
3. Eating their food cold; for they always let their boiled meat cool before they taste it, and do not seize it with avidity as soon as it comes out of the pot.
4. The purity of the water.
5. Tranquillity of mind. (...)
6. Their never overloading the stomach, while the rustic of other countries eats till he is ready to burst.
7. Deficiency of spirituous liquors. (...)
8. Their being inured to cold from their infancy renders them hardy.
9. Probably the quantity of flesh they eat may prolong their lives, as carnivorous animals are long-lived.

[Linné1, pg. 334]

...just till over there!

Day 8 | July, 23ʳᵈ:
Bridge across Gådokjåhkå | 2ⁿᵈ Rest Day

It's raining. We hear the rainfall on our tent roof all the day playing a symphony of melancholy humility towards the powers of nature in different tones. Sometimes like waves and quiet, sometimes hard and dribbling. The dependency from the weather hits us directly and forces us to decide, whether to continue the hike or not. There is nothing in between.

The mountain tops are vanished in low-lying clouds. The sky is completely cloudy, only 2 or 3 times the sun breaks hopefully through for seconds. However, there is a celestial cooking top syndrome above us. It doesn't make any sense to do any bigger thing today.

I start again taking some pictures and on the way back I bring another few remains of the side boards of the concrete pylons. I am going to peel patiently more scraps of bark skin off the birch logs for good half an hour and actually make it to light the rain-soaked boards. The second half of yesterday's salami feeds the stomachs slightly. We pour chicken soup with noodles and semolina dumplings on top. Finally, we abondon ourselves to digestion for the rest of the day – more or less noisily.

This Kind of Solid Food is a Dream

Day 9 | July, 24th:
Daytrip to Rapaätno

This morning again the rain determines the coming events. The sun peers sporadically through the dark clouds. In any case we are obliged to move – comes what may.

The sky looks as if he would end the shame and brightens. Finally he does and we prepare for being at the ready. Some items are put into Niklas's backpack, because this one is the smallest: 2 x 20 m of rope, 5 m of tubular tape (for possibly tying a chest strap) wading sandals for each of us and rain suits, if massif rain would come as a surprise over us. We will be on tour for some hours. The one-way distance amounts 8 – 9 km.

The aim today is Rapaätno, the great river, which crosses Sarek from the northwest corner to southeast one. We are going to check, whether there is a possibility to cross the river. If yes, we could choose a different way back to Saltoluokta. Then we would walk along the northern bank of the Rapa in direction to east and finish at Aktse fjällstation, by taking a motorboat transfer for the last part of the way through the picturesque delta of the Rapa river. Otherwise we will be forced to take the same way back we came from.

We cross over „our" Gådokjåhkå bridge and keep left beneath the elongated flank of the Gådokgájsse. There is much of bush vegetation with walking impairment on two thirds of the distance between Gådokgájsse and the river that goes parallel to the mountain flank through a narrow canyon until it reaches the treeline in Rapadalen. Thus says the map. We plan to pass the bush vegetation 50 m above on the mountain flank keeping the green stuff untouched below us, till crossing the water course coming down the peak of Gådokgájsse some 1670 m high. We want to descent along its shores down to the valley of the Rapaätno.

In this moment we are about 900 m high, the 2 km wide willow belt gets up to 950 m. The option of taking the upper way also means a longer distance. Although we virtually have no luggage with us – except some little things in Niklas's backpack – we choose against our better judgement the willow-option, hoping that future will probably be not that bad.

Far from it, with the choice of the best alternative we – of course – draw the ultimate blank: willows, willows and even more willows as far as the eye can see. We walk ankle-deep in water over long distances. The walking comfort is none – the tenacious and intractable willows win more than one battle, when you try to trample them down. Here we have "**swamp complete**".

Even the absence of any luggage doesn't make it easier to work on such tough terrain. It is very exhausting. Lastly, not far before the height, from which the path descents to the valley, the soil becomes wonderful underfoot.

Sometimes the Skierffe comes into view on the right hand side (far towards the east) and a glimpse on the winding Rapaätno. It doesn't take long that the Nammatj rock, guarding the Rapa delta like a block or better said like a stone wedge pushes its way into the picture to full format. This is a completely new point of view for Jens and my own and Niklas, too, is thrilled about this marvelous panorama. Far in the background the Laitaure glistens invitingly. Laitaure was our second rowing lake.

Reaching the contour line of 700 m we cross the treeline. Almost immediately below us a thick birch tree jungle arises reaching down to the Rapa. We are forced to penetrate this jungle for a distance of 1,5 to 2 km. The vegetation is immense: flowers, ferns, grasses and the typical birch trees - everything is available in abundance.

The first 60 meters height within this arctic Matto Grosso descent steeply. It becomes necessary to concentrate the own attention towards walking, because the special delicacy here is, that one walks quasi-blind. The rich cloak of vegetation is covering everything: stones, smooth surfaced roots, fallen trees, holes in the soil. It is the purest obstacle course. After a while we cross a game path. Fresh tracks and plenty of droppings of elks indicate it as an elk-highway. We follow the trail and find out, that

> *Birch trees were to be found even on the highest part of this hill, but of a very diminutive stature. Their trunks were thick but low, and their highest shoots seemed to have been killed by frost, so that the young leaves looked as if they were growing out of branches that had been burnt. I was told that these trees afford every year but a very small portion of sap, and that the wood is much harder than the common kind. Such diminutive trees grow to a[Pg 272] great age. The further I proceeded up the country, the smaller I still found them.*
>
> *[Linné1, pg. 271f]*

walking on game paths means a comparably comfortable alternative to our self-chosen attempts passing through the green wall. As there are tons of those hardly visible trails it is worth to reckon one or the other supposed detour. On the bottom line doing this one will move more quickly and above all saving much efforts.

...just till over there!

Indeed the vegetation is extremely dense. In the north the treeline is mainly determined by the mountain birch tree (*Betula tortulosa*).

On the high plains you will often find wide areas of willows (*Salix*), taking up the one or the other hectare from time to time.

Carl von Linné coined the term **Limes norrlandicus** (also *biological boundary of the Northland*), which means the biological boundary between mixed forests in the south and coniferous boreal forests in the north, i.e. Norrland. Driving through Lapland one sees above all pine-, spruce- and birch tree forests, but also willows and crane-trees. Environmental factors like temperature differences, extremely changing solar radiation und snow storms have an impact on all lifecycle phases of the flora there. In Lapland you can find among other things seas of flowers and one of the best-known berry of the north: the cloudberry (*Hjortron [swed.] or Lakka [fin.]*), known by the locals as "marsh gold".

Alas, we stumble on several kilos of elk droppings, but will never meet face to face one of the separators of this oval, pressed shit that looks like rolled tobacco, when such a "suppository" will be broken in half. What we now have is the dry summer shit in contrast to the mushy winter shit. Other representatives of the fauna are disappearing, too. And yet we would like to go out hunting for bears – as the ancient Laplanders did (*see next box*). Can't be that difficult, if you believe in old stories. Finally, the bear population has been increased during the last years, after the teddy bears had vanished completely in between times. Of course you should be very careful, if you were in luck to see a real-life bear. Getting as far away as possible is first civic duty.

Or would it just be better to put Hubertus into the pocket going for bears? Crafting a rifle will not necessarily be easy to realize. But what about a bow? Some years ago, Niklas gave it a try with a blank. But from a single kind of wood. The result was not bad. But it would be much better to choose a combination of two or even more timbers with different properties. The "only" thing is to combine them. It's no big problem, if you know how to do it (*see next box*).

Well, at the final count, I think the bears are safe from us. We would be satisfied with a smaller prey. After all we can proudly present a trained hunter with Niklas, who could cut up the prey in compliance with the hunting principles.

We do not waste time by thinking about that topic any longer, but direct our steps towards the mountain Lulep Spádnek on the other bank of the

...just till over there!

Rapaätno. After countless slides over hidden roots, depth measurements of overgrown holes in the earth and stumbling sportive entertainments over steep parts of the path, only stopped by well-meaning birch trees, we finally reach the lifeline of the Sarek. It goes seamlessly out of the jungle and directly onto the stony bank of the Rapa. I am glad having reached the goal and can make a long break now.

> The glue used by the Laplanders for joining the two portions of different woods of which their bows are made (see p. 66,) is prepared from the Common Perch (Perca fluviatilis) in the following manner. Some of the largest of this fish being flayed, the skins are first dried, and afterwards soaked in a small quantity of cold water, so that the scales can be rubbed off. Four or five of these skins being wrapped up together in a bladder, or in a piece of birch bark, so that no water can get at them, are set on the fire in a pot of water to boil, a stone being laid over the pot, to keep in the heat. The skins thus prepared make a very strong glue, insomuch that the articles joined with it will never separate again. A bandage is tied round the bow while making, to hold the two parts the more firmly together.
>
> [Linné2, pg. 86f]

Bright sunshine lets the river appear it all of its beauty and the now undrowned and dry rocks due to the low water level shine brightly. Despite of the relative low water level the riverbed is about 40 to 50 meters wide. There is significantly deep water with strong current in the middle of the river. Crossing here is impossible. Upstream the map shows a small island in the river. From our present location, the distance between the island and the other bank seems not to be a problem. But from this side of the Rapa to the island the distance grows with every step that we come closer. There will always remain a part of some meters of bubbling current that is impassable. We spend some efforts on looking for a crossover for the next 2 km, but either near the bank or in the middle of the river, there are always some meters so deep and powerful that every attempt to cross here with full baggage would be out of culpable imprudence.

Herewith the planned alternate route back along the other bank to the beginning of the delta and making the last part to Aktse by motorboat with Lennart, the Expensive, has become obsolete. Now we are forced to take the same way back that we came. Other routes would outgrow our timeframe.

The refreshing water an armlength away we enjoy the warmth of the sun for a while, before we start to return to our base camp. It goes up right next to the Gådokjágásj for getting as soon as possible out of the forest. Again the elk crossings are a great help in this affair. Alas, again we are not in luck to face one of the carriers of big antlers.

The way back stretches like chewing gum. During the last hour my back hurts extremely. Maybe the reason is the bundle of small twigs I was desperately clinching with my right hand for not loosing a single branch-let. I need the brushwood and the pocket full of thin birch tree bark for blowing the fire lateron. Salami sends its best.

After 7 hours and 15 km we touch the tent. I am heavily exhausted, slip out of my gaiters, shoes and socks and disappear in my sleeping bag.

Aaaah, stretching my legs – what a wonderful feeling. My partners are doing the same.

> Hunting the Bear is often undertaken by a single man, who, having discovered the retreat of the animal, takes his dog along with him (...). The jaws of the dog are tied round with a cord, to prevent his barking (...). As soon as the dog smells the bear, he begins to show signs of uneasiness, and by dragging at the cord informs his master that the object of his pursuit is at no great distance. When the Laplander by this means discovers on which side the bear is stationed, he advances in such a direction that the wind may blow from the bear to him, and not the contrary; (...) When he has gradually advanced to within gunshot of the bear, he fires upon him (...). Should the man chance to miss his aim, the furious beast will directly turn upon him in a rage, and the little Laplander is obliged to take to his heels with all possible speed, leaving his knapsack behind him on the spot. The bear coming up with this, seizes upon it, biting and tearing it into a thousand pieces. While he is thus venting his fury, and bestowing all his attention, upon the knapsack, the Laplander takes the opportunity of loading his gun, and firing a second time; when he is generally sure of hitting the mark, and the bear either falls upon the spot or runs away.
>
> [Linné2, pg. 84f]

One should have to be physically fit as a Laplander. Seems, that nothing could kill them. At least, believing Carl von Linné, who was in the mountains for a whole day with two old Laplanders (70 and 50 years old) during his Lapland-Expedition in 1732. In the evening he wondered, that his companions were so agil although they carried the complete luggage all day long. He was deeply impressed by that excellent fitness, which he looked somewhat enviously at and searched for the reasons of this astonishing fact (*see information in the next box*).

...just till over there!

F. l. t. r.: Skierffe, Nammatj and Lake Laitaure

The Green Cloudy Stuff is „Bush Vegetation"

Hunger is slowly taken root, what occasionally leads to strange behavior. Or why does my son looks at me in that strange manner, when I point to my hat pulled over the footend of my sleeping bag, which I let friendly nodding by moving my feet to and fro? But I'm not yet talking to my socks…

Jens, the tireless expedition cook, buckles down again and creates a culinary delicacy conjuring up from the depth of our provisions: with a cube of fat broth refined spiralling noodles – in a considerable quantity. For dessert we have chocolate hazelnut spread with cereal bars. In addition to that Niklas stands us generously pieces of „his" lactose free chocolate as Jens and I had destroyed our "normal" chocolate completely.

Now, peace and tranquility reigns in the tent, apart from diverse noises, which can be broadly associated with digestion activities. In former times, Luther would have stated this more clearly!

...just till over there!

The final completion of this wonderful day includes the assassination of perceived another some millions mosquitos and the random distribution of their powdered bodies anywhere. Remorselessly! Bastards!

This set me seriously to consider the question (...)"why are the Laplanders so swift-footed?" (...)

1. The Laplanders, unlike us, wear no heels to their half boots (..) on the contrary, those who are accustomed to large and high heels, move in a heavy and deliberate manner. (...). Those muscles, by means of high heels, and consequently less use or exercise, become more and more stiff, and a man with a wooden foot or leg cannot but move heavily.

2. These people are accustomed to running from their infancy. As soon as a Lapland boy can go alone, he is taught to run and put a halter round the reindeer's neck. When he grows a little older, he learns to follow these animals, which are always quick-paced (...).

3. Freedom from hard labour is another cause. All laborious employments, such as directing the plough, threshing, cutting and hewing of wood, &c. render the blood thick, and the limbs stiff (...) nor can a peasant move with the lightness and flexibility (...). The Laplanders appear to be more nimble and active, in all their movements, because they undergo no hard or Herculean labours.

4. Habitual exercise of the muscles. A rope-dancer trains his pupils to the continual contraction and dilatation of their muscles, that they may acquire the more pliability. (...) So the Laplanders are perpetually exercising the muscles used in walking, (...) that they are able to sit for a long while cross-legged, without pain or inconvenience (...).

5. Animal food. (...) The Laplanders are altogether carnivorous. (...) They now and then indeed eat a raw stalk of Angelica (...) and occasionally a few leaves of Sorrel (...). In spring they eat fish, in winter nothing but meat, in summer milk and its various preparations. (...)

6. The Laplander is satisfied with a small quantity of food at once. He does not eat his fill at one meal, but takes food from time to time, as he feels inclined. (...) [Linné1, pg. 326ff]

Day	distance km	meters up + down	start Level	end Level	peaks, rivers, lakes on the way
9	16	800	900	900	Gadokvagge Lulep Spatnek (816 m) Gadokvaratj (902 m) Rapaätno
Cumulated Values	74	2635			

...just till over there!

Day 10 | July, 25th:
Daytrip to Gådoktjåkkåh

It is raining again during the night. With monotonous regularity. Seems, the high mountains surround, which hem our area leaving only the south line open, are the reason for that. In the morning the sky brightens. In spots in the true sense of the words, blue sky is to be seen. We take the occasion of a 3-minute-sunshine-sequence for a quick bath in the glacial river.

The routinely prepared breakfast does not show any tasty surprises, either. In the end you will be glad having gulped your pot of muesli successfully.

While eating we sit upon the today's tour goal. As the weather promises to stay more or less dry, we decide for the ascent of our backyard mountain Gådoktjåhkkå. This massif consists of several ridges and tops reaching up to 1978 m.

The cold, but dry wind will not stop us from doing this trip. We cross the bridge and at first follow the run-off of the small glacier situated directly

> *A stream of happiness is running through my bosom and nobody knows me sitting on this barren rock.*
> *[Hamsun, pg. 954]*

beneath a nameless peak of 1885 m. The as well nameless glacial river ends in the Gådokjåhkå close to our bridge.

The first part of the ascent leads over soft soil interspersed with rocks and stones and is wonderful underfoot. This does not change for more than 2 km up to a height of about 1100 m (the bridge is almost precisely situated at 900 m altitude). Then it becomes steeper and after 1200 m even steeper and unexceptional stony. Slip rocks as far as the eye can reach. Only very occasionally a solitary plant is peeping out of the grey stones.

The wind is rather strong. We are now at the east wall of Gådokgájsse, which has a peak on 1670 m. When we reach a sub-peak with its 1524 m, we are all together. At least 1 km only is missing till the end of the incision, where the last hurdle in the form of an even steeper ascent for more than 350 meters in height is waiting for us.

„Well, the peak over there is worth a visit", Niklas says pointing to the 1670 m peak. "When I am here anyhow I want to look at the other side."

This is an interesting idea in itself, as the ascent from our current position (1524 m) up is less easygoing and in addition to that there will 150 steep meters in height less to be mastered. On the other hand romping amidst middle sized boulders is too vigorous in the long run. Jens and I decide to re-descent 50 m and to cover the last kilometer over the big snowfield that reaches till the end of the mentioned incision, and then climbing to the greatest height today.

Although it is not the less strenuous tramping through the snow, but is a bit more comfortable than walking through boulders, where you ought to think about each step for not stumbling. Niklas appears regularly on the ridge, demonstrating where he currently is located. We signal to meet him, where the last part of the ascent up to 1885 m begins. This last effort we want to master in partnership. And thus, it's going to happen.

„You should have gone with me. I had a fantastic view into the Rapa-dalen, on Skierffe and Nammatj and on the far away delta. It was great!"

Niklas is deeply impressed by his detour. Now we are going to master the last 200 meters in height. That's not half bad. This ascent robs my strength. Through narrow serpentines I am winding slowly upwards. The weather has become worse in the meanwhile. Sleety rain has joined the wind not really supporting our well-being.

And then yes, we are finally on top at 1885 m – we climbed nearly 1000 meters in height, only to descent back in the same moment. How crazy could one be? Why are we doing all this?

But turning around and looking on some of the 200 summits in Sarek, I actually know the reason. The view is overwhelming! We are on the second highest point of this massif now. In the west we can see the steep wall of Skájdetjåhkkå abundantly provided with snowfields, only separated by the narrow Jiegnavágge from Gådoktjåhkkå. Far in the east we get a glimpse of Rapadalen. Niklas had that already a little more clearly in focus. In the south there is the open high plain of Ijvvárlahko and a bit to the west of it the Bårdde-Massif raises with the impressive glacier Bårddejiegna, clinging with its "fingers" as a giant ice-hand to the cliff. Along with it there are Bårddetjåhkkå, Bálgattjåhkkå and Lullihatjåhkkå (all about 2000 m high), blocking the view to far west, in direction to Padjelanta, „the higher land" as it is named by the Sami people. Far in the north, within the Sarektjåhkkå-Massif, the highest summits in Sarek Nationalpark can be seen: Stortoppen (2089m) and Sydtoppen together with Nordtoppen (2023 m). Against this our tiny tent is impossibly to recognize. It is 6 to 7 kilometers away from here.

...just till over there!

The Scandinavian Mountains (also named *Skanden*; or Swedish *Fjällen*) extend from the Norwegian Skagerrak in south till the Nordkapp. The mountain chain is of a length of approximately 1.700 km and a wideness of 320 km at a max. Norway and Sweden have the biggest stake in these mountains, which mark the national border between these two countries. Additionally the Skanden are the continental divide in the northern area of Scandinavia.

Geologically mountain range arose approximately 420 – 380 million years ago. When Pangäa, the supercontinent; broke up and plate tectonics was in full swing, the Canadian Shield and the Baltic Shield collided and formed the so-called Caledonian Mountains with the Skanden as a part of it. During the ice age the Skanden were sheeted with ice 1500 meters thick. In the following aeons the glacial polish has led to round and soft mountain shapes, rather than pronounced peaks. These can be found only in the Norwegian part in Jotunheimen (with Europe's biggest mainland glacier Jostedalsbreen) and in the Swedish Sarek Nationalpark. In Jotunheimen the Skanden present Galdhøpiggen (2.469 m high) as the highest point of Northern Europe. Kebnekaise is the highest mountain in Sweden with its 2.111 m. Nowhere else in Scandinavia today's mountains crack the mark of 2000 meters.

Today, finally, I can fulfil my mission! Right before the start of the journey, my friend Oliver with whom I made my first tours in Lapland, wished me a nice trip via email message and asking me jokingly for raising one of those typical "stonemen" you may find in the mountain scape. This opportunity could not have come at a better time. Days before I saw this action before my mind's eye: a message, wrapped into an empty film container, should have been left for posterity and the whole stuff must be documented photographically.

Now it happens exactly that way. Ice cold fingers install a small – about 40 cm tall – stoneman on the today's highest peak of 1885 m. I prepared the message during the past few days and kept the film can in my pocket this morning.

And this is the message (*see next page*):

...just till over there!

Immediately after this pioneering activity – the fingers still numb from cold – we start going back without further delay, first of all to get off the strong wind. In this moment we are on a ridge above that snowfield, Jens and I walked upon till the end of the valley some time ago.

In the first instance it is still stony, of course, but after the first 400 meters in height the path leads steadily downwards. The tailpiece goes over nicely covered soil. It seems this one is very popular to the reindeer. Usually we should see one herd beside another – if not here, where else? But in reality we haven't got a glimpse at a single biologically packed reindeer bacon. Only reindeerless antlers are richly available. I clean up the landscape and collect a dozen of small antlers – single poles -, which will serve for decoration purposes at home lateron.

That was a nice tour – exhausting, but nice. We went up 1000 meters in height and the same down. This is a good reason for imbibing the next salami in good conscience.

...just till over there!

Raising Olli's Stoneman

End of a Glissade

Day	distance km	meters up + down	start Level	end Level	peaks, rivers, lakes on the way
10	14	1960	900	900	Peak 1524 m Gadoktjakka (1885 m) Piellorieppe (1830 m) Unna Stuolo (1766 m) Skaitetjakka (1933 m) Gadokkaise (1670 m)
Cumulated Values	88	4595			

...just till over there!

Day 11 | July, 26th:
Bridge across Gådokjåhkå | 3rd Rest Day

Lazy day! Sleeping until the break of day we nearly miss the obligatory muesli-breakfast. Flexible people are not struggling with loss of opportunities, but prepare chip potatoes for brunch. The precooked potatoes are one of our weighty food components. Due to that those culinary and caloric highlights are provided only for a limited number of days.

The potatoes are being upgraded. No, not by using fat broth but – who would have thought it – with salami, which is being roasted over open fire simultaneously to the sizzling potatoes. The birch tree bark I collected in the woods of the Rapaätno yesterday and a hand full of brush wood serve as a perfect firestarter.

Round bellies, rich feelings! Jens is sprawling in the landscape with camping mat and sleeping bag and begins reading his book. This year he brought with him „Water Music" (by T. C. Boyle). Niklas is squatting on a rock, drawing a picture of our tent. And I'm going to make again a little photo safari. It remains dry the whole day long.

Later, we make an inventory of our provisions. The result is that we still have 11 warm meals for 9 coming days. Niklas and I consider economically justified the surplus to be reinvested without any delay into our bodys' own energy balances. To say it clearly: instead of getting served the skipped muesli breakfast we vote vehemently for a big portion of Asia-Noodles. Blessed be, what is filling me.

A census of antlers is still pending, being bound up with a selection of what should be taken home. At least we have collected a huge bulk of them.

But nobody likes to do anything on a full stomach. Perhaps we will do it tomorrow, when we will have returned from our daytrip to Bårddejiegna. Its ice-front reaches far into the valley close enough to touch just 7 km ahead. Thus says the map. Bårddetjåhkkå with its proud altitude of 2005 m is the highest peak in the area und simultaneously one of the highest-ever peaks in Sarek.

...just till over there!

Day 12 | July, 27th:
Daytrip to Bårddejiegna

All is dry, everything is well. The daytrip to the glacier can take place. We allow ourselves a good deal of time – after all we are on our holidays – and start at half past eleven. For the first time since we came here I put on a knee cuff as a precaution as I'm expecting a total distance between 17 and 20 km including some ascents and descents. Up to now I haven't had any problems with my operated meniscus. The knee-doctors had done an excellent job.

A light cloudy sky letting the sun shine through now and then provides a friendly-pleasant atmosphere. Starting on this side of the river – i.e. no bridge crossing – we follow the Gådkokjåhkkå in westerly direction firstly over mild slopes. There is a lonely, locked Sami hut nearby (Renvaktarstuga) we pass on the way to the glacier.

Little by little – over a distance of 6 km – we get from 900 to 1100 meters in height. Whilst this, some smaller creeks want to be skipped over. The mountain Lullihatjárro with its just 1586 m comes closer and closer. Directly behind in direction of march the glacier advances its ice-front till the middle of the its flank.

About 3 km north of Lulllihatjárro the Gaskastjåhkkå climbs up to 1825 m. You can choose here, whether to pass him on the western side aiming to Lullihavágge or on the eastern side aiming to Gaskasvágge for reaching the crossing Sarvesvágge lateron. According to our originally planned route we would have come from the north through Lullihavágge for raising the base camp exactly on the place, where it actually is now.

The weather is clear. All the mountains show their impressive splendor. Everywhere around we can see dark mountain flanks decorated with snowfields. The landscape has changed completely. The soft overgrown waves in the Earth's crust are yielded naked rock. We are currently right below one of the steep slopes of Boarektjåhkkå (1805 m). This one has collected a vast deposit of scree at its foot. It seems one can follow erosion here live and in color. In the bottom of the valley more and more parts of scree mix with bigger rocks lying around unmotivated. There are virtually no plants to be seen.

We come to realize that map and reality do not match (any longer). The ice-front of the glacier on our map does currently not exist in the shown dimensions. Since the printing of the map (2009) the glacier has been

...just till over there!

melted away for estimated 3 km (!). Currently we walk on the bottom of the valley, which is – as a geological aspect – freshly freed from ice and experience „up close", what it looks like beneath a glacier.

Gravel, scree, finely crushed crumbs of stones as far as the eye can reach. Plenty of small bumps and depressions remind of a sector of the front in World War I. The only thing missing is the barb wire. A desolation, which is unbeatable. It is deathly quiet. Not a single breeze blows. The only noise comes from beneath the interspersed snowfields and remaining sheets of ice, where snowmelt is murmuring softly.

> Indeed I was now, for the first time, upon the Alps! Snowy mountains encompassed me on every side. I walked in snow, as if it had been the severest winter.
>
> *[Linné1, pg. 284]*
>
> The lofty mountains, piled one upon another, showed no signs of volcanic fire, but were covered with stones, all of a fissile kind, and by that means easily distinguishable.
>
> *[Linné1, pg. 291]*

Since the birth of the mountains millions of years ago erosion has done its best. The glaciers of the last ice age have made only a small contribution to the planation. The biggest erosion was made by wind and weather during the incredible long periods of time, which passed by since the formation of Scandinavia. Only the youngest of several mountain ranges arisen one after the other, does exist nowadays, known as „Caledonian Mountains". Anything else has vanished. Weathered and levelled. It is estimated that the height of the removed rock crust was 10 kilometers – and this is a rather reserved estimate. Probably, there was even more.

Who is walking in Scandinavia on rocks polished by the ice, does it inmidst ancient, eroded mountains. In this region airliners fly, where once the summits had been.

Nevertheless, despite all roughness there is life even here. Jens discovers a mountain fox, the fjällräven, on a snowfield 200 m ahead. In his summer coat, he gallops over the snow, pauses once looking in our direction and vanishes between the numerous rocks lying around here.

We re-orient. Bårddejiegna possesses 5 fingers. From our base camp one can see the most northern and thickest one and its neighbour. These are surrounded by almost vertical flanks Lullihatjåhkkå (1940 m), Tvillingryggen (1846 m) and Balgattjåhkkå (2002 m). In the meantime we have nearly reached the foothills of Balgattjåhkkå, without having walked over snow or ice. That far the glacier has melted.

We must have already passed the place, where according to the map a moderate ascent along the eastern edge of the charted glacier should be possible as we oriented towards the real glacier. We planned to ascent along the edge of the ice and look for the solitary „Pårtetjåkkå Observatorium" on the mountain's ridge. Now we are far beyond this place and nearly reached the end of the valley. Perhaps we can find another way up onto the ridge that connects the surrounding summits. Then we could go up there in easterly direction back to the tent. In this case we would inevitably pass the observatory.

The relative gently rising Balgattjåhkkå lends itself as ascent. But will one have reached the ridge, a snowbridge about 30 – 50 m wide, breaks the stony back and falls away sharply to the flank facing us. It is probably the same on the other side. The width of the snow- resp. ice ridge cannot be more than 2 meters. This seems highly dangerous and not calculable.

We dally over the middle „finger". It seems to be feasible here to get up via the northern slope. It will become damned steep in the final section, but mostly it will go over scree. Thus, we will give it a try.

We manage the first half without any problems. Where once was the glacier its debris like legacy let us unspectacularly gasping up 400-500 meters in height in self-chosen serpentines until we stand in front of the steeply rising final slope. For studying these last 300-400 meters in height you need to put your head significantly back.

Bloody hell – but giving up now?

In between, i.e. at two-thirds of this Jacob's Ladder, there are some sustainded snowfields, which could possibly be helpful. Jens precedes and with his sturdy hiking shoes he makes steps into the snow Niklas and I use as a staircase. Things are going slowly getting up. The very last piece of way leads us again over rocks and large-sized scree.

As in earlier times in Norway on the narrow Besseggen Ridge we were forced to lend a hand permanently – it was too steep.

We do not climb in a vertical line but go off-centered for avoiding the man below getting in closer contact with a rock possibly set off by the ones above him. Once, Niklas pushes a big stone in my direction, but fortunately its kinetic energy is not sufficient to let it leave its position definitely.

Now and then a rock prepares for beginning to slide, but regularly remains in the small scree.

Then we are finally on top, directly next to a fat stonepile, which marks the highest point in this environment. The effort was worth it. The view is clear, not only on the nearest mountains. In the distance we can identify the high peaks of Sarektjåhkkå, such as Nord-, Syd- and Stortoppen, which are the highest Sarek summits, although there is a blanket of clouds above our heads.

The panoramic view is fantastic. We enjoy it for a good while before we are going to start the way back. However, not without putting an additional stone on top of the fat stonepile.

Snow Ridge at the Balgattjåhkkå

We look forward with eager anticipation to the observatory we must pass by walking along the edges of the glacier's „fingers". We were in luck with the timing: while reaching the summit a wide blanket of clouds has been deployed, but it was high enough to allow looking into the far below the clouds. Now, they fall steadily and appear as fog at higher altitudes. Soon the view isn't borderless any longer, but is limited after one or two dozens of meters.

The observatory was raised by Axel Hamberg, who studies the Sarek over 4 decades – as already mentioned above. Thus, he was the proverbial expert in this affair. In this observatory scientific examinations of the Sarek mountains had been done. It was built in the early years of the 20th century – precisely in 1911. The material must had been carried on the backs of the researchers. In total, Hamberg had raised 5 of these observatories in the Sarek mountains. Axel Hamberg developed these tin sheds by himself. The climatic and geological conditions in the Lap mountains as well as the flora had been analyzed here.

Besides that, in 1922 Axel Hamberg wrote the first Sarek guide titled „Sarek-fjällen", which was published by the STF.

> We undertook to cross the ice-mountain. Having proceeded some way on our journey, we observed a dense cloud to the north-east. It was visible both above and below us, and at length approached us in the form of a thick mist, which moistened our clothes, and rendered even our hair thoroughly wet. It so completely obliterated our horizon, that we could neither see sun nor moon, nor the summits of the neighbouring hills. We knew not whither to turn our steps, fearing on the one hand to fall down a precipice and lose our lives (...). Our situation was like that of an unskilful mariner at sea without a compass, out of sight of land, and surrounded by hidden rocks on every side. The Laplanders themselves consider the situation we were in as one of the worst accidents that can ever befall them. We, however, though destitute of a guide, were fortunate enough to discover the track of a reindeer (...). This track directed us safely to one of the Lapland moveable tents.
>
> *[Linné2, pg. 5]*

In brief, we do not find the observatory. Jens supposes the „Kjöttbullar-kneaders" are kidding us. We probably moved to close to the cliff edge and the fog went one step further. Well, it wasn't meant to be.

The distance left between the observatory and the expected röstis for supper is about 10 km and 900 meters in height. Here it goes!

Fog

...just till over there!

Stepmaker Jens

Meet us on Top!

...just till over there!

Even on top of the ridge there is no solid rock, but also only brash and crumbly debris. The shoes are wet from snow we strode through generously – and little by little the feet get cold. We step out quickly hoping the feet will get warm again.

> We determined to seek for a Laplander's hut. In order to get at one, we were obliged to descend so steep a hill, that, being unable to walk down it, I lay down on my back and slid along, with the rapidity of an arrow from a bow.
> [Linné2, pg.2]

We follow the elongated ridge. Even being in the mist that is actually no problem, because it doesn't keep on falling from a certain height. Thus, the view improves with any further meter descending. Soon we can look far to the south again. Before Boarektjåhkkå a swamp- and lake area over and over again interrupted from forests spreads in green and blue colors around the settlement Parek. The view is open till Kvikkjokk, which is the starting or terminal point of the middle part of Kungsleden and has road connection.

In march direction the complete high plain Ijvvárlahko raises behind our base camp and in this moment we have an overview of the possible routes we can choose the day after tomorrow for bypassing the bloody bush vegetation.

The last 600 meters in height upwards are very simple as at least two thirds of them are made by sliding over snow fields. This is mere fun! We do not drop any proper snow field for this action. Being down in the valley we again stroll slowly over soft and well passable soil. Jens and

> The fire-places here were furnished with a regular apparatus for boiling the kettle. The Laplanders in general content themselves for this purpose with a large stick, which they place obliquely in the ground, so as to lean over the fire, and on which they suspend either a kettle or a fish (...).
> [Linné1, pg. 198]

Niklas are ahead during the last 2-3 km. I follow at a slower pace, but therefore I have the leisure to discover all the reindeer antlers in the surroundings bleached by wind and weather. I do, what I have to do and tidy up the fjäll. Another 4 small antlers will complete the collection.

This spectacular trip lasted nearly 9 hours. We covered a distance of more than 24 km and more than 2000 meters in height. That is justification enough for being allowed to be exhausted.

Jens and I take a quick bath for rinsing the sweat. I take this opportunity and the friendly weather to pull shirt, trousers and underwear through the water. It's useless, I know – the stuff is still stinking as if one has mopped a puma cage. The lassitude helps to strengthen the indifference towards the mosquitos. Oh, let them bite…

Back at the tent Jens handles the outdoor-kitchen in a virtuous manner again, knipling simultaneously on 2 cookers in 3 pots röstis for all. Parallel to that I fan the flame and together with my son we roast a quarter of a salami as an addition to the röstis We dine at the open fire and enjoy the meal we really deserve. Entirely full and satisfied we lay down, bracing up only for guzzling hot tea into the superior body orifice.

There is nothing more to do. Jens tries to read in his book in the fading daylight, while Niklas is already residing in Morpheus's arms.

After some tea induced tinkle stunts it is deadly quiet inside the tent.

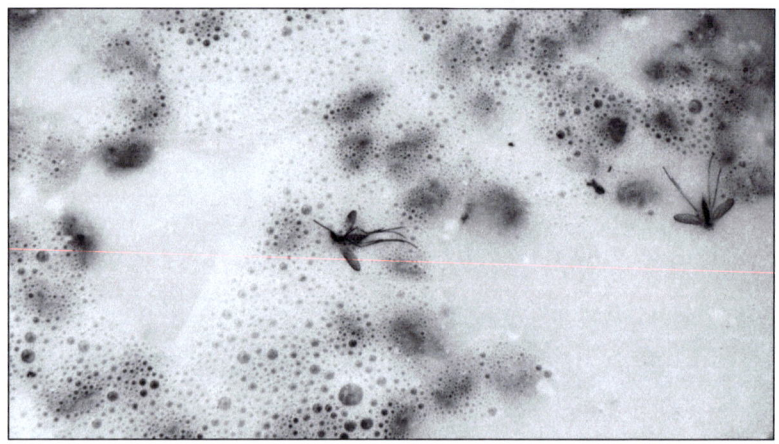

Muesli with added „Meat"

Day	distance km	meters up + down	start Level	end Level	peaks, rivers, lakes on the way
12	24	2210	900	900	Skaitetjakka (1933 m) Lullihatjarro (1586 m) Parektjaka (1805 m) Lullihatjakka (1940 m) Tvillingryggen (1846 m) Balgattjakka (2002 m) Barddetjakka (2005 m) Glacier Barddejegna
Cumulated Values	112	6805			

...just till over there!

Day 13 | July, 28th:
Bridge across Gådokjåhkå | 4th Rest Day

The plan for today was housekeeping: clearing up, winnowing the stock of antlers, preparing packing the backpacks etc, etc. But heavy and continuous rain prevents us from doing this.

It is not until about noon that the rain ceases and anytime it stops completely what allows us yet again to dry some things in the open air.

The rest of the day supplies an event: from the flour mixture, that we have commandeered in

> *Scarcely any other fish is found in the lakes of this neighbourhood than the Röding, which the Laplanders call Raud (Salmo alpinus, or Charr), and this is extremely abundant. It is a Salmon, or rather Trout, with a scarlet belly. Its length is about a foot. The scales are extremely minute. Head smooth, ovate, obtuse. Jaws furnished with teeth, and the tongue also bears two rows of teeth, six in each row.*   *[Linné1, pg. 306]*

Rittak we create some further „Vindskydd-Bratlinge" baked in generously given fat. Those are crumbled in fat broth and eaten as big croutons.

Yum yum!

One day Niklas experimented with a miserable fishing gear (only cord and hook), what, of course, was not crowned with success. Such a fresh swimmer would have been a welcome change.

Alas, we had immense misfortune concerning encounters with reindeer. In this year 2012 we didn't see a single one, even less a herd, where one could have gained a pot of milk by trickery.

> *One of the Laplanders' dishes, called Kappi, or Kappa-tialmas, is pre-pared in the following manner. While the milk of the reindeer, intended for making cheese, is warm, before the rennet is added to it, a film rises to the top, which is taken off carefully with a spoon, and put into the bladder of a reindeer. This is hung up against the side of the hut to dry; after which it is eaten, being esteemed a great delicacy. They frequently mix some kind of berries with it when used. The fruit called Hjortron, (Cloud-berry, or Rubus Chamæmorus,) bruised and eaten with milk of the reindeer, is also a very palatable Lapland dish.*
>
> *[Linné1, pg. 282]*

Day 14 | July, 29th:
Bridge across Gådokjåhkå – Vindskydd Rittak

Rain! Plenty of rain! The whole night through. And even longer. None of us really wants to get up.

„Oh, oh, we're going to drown!" Jens's sudden interjection has the effect of an electric shock.

Indeed! The complete ground sheet is soaking wet. And all of our camping mats and sleeping bags, too, where they have had contact to the ground sheet. The same applies to several other things having laid at the foot end of the mats.

Instantly, we are fully awake and firstly place all things lying around anywhere on the mats. Then we start the packing sequence urgently, but not hectically.

The tent stands on a step in the terrain. The heavy and permanent rain has created a runlet that has grown in overcoming several steps in the terrain. As a climax it flows right through the living room now.

The rain has stopped at this moment. But the clouds are very low and cut the summits of all surrounding mountains at one level. We continue packing up the equipment. Finally, the wet tent is going to be stowed away in my backpack. Now, it is weighing probably 2 kg more than in dry state. The rope, too, being used as a laundry line has soaked to its double weight.

It is muggy. The grey clouds are still low. We are going to protect us against further downpours from above and start the today's stage fully rigged with rain jackets and rain trousers.

This time the route shall NOT run through the swampy bush vegetation, but more to the east, above the green stuff. We want the way back to Saltoluokta being slow-paced and thus plan to spent the night after about 6 km at the slope of Suolanjunnje (1088 m). Tomorrow the planning says to walk another 6 km till the vindskydd Rittak. Depending on our mood and the weather we will decide, whether to stay there for the night or not.

The stage is not older than only 2 minutes, when I desperately must get rid of my jacket. The sweat is running down in streams and my constitution is going to be virtually zero. The others nearly feel the same. Don't know what the cause is. Well, in any case we will continue shirt-sleeved.

However, we do not manage to avoid the swamp and the willows. Again we are shuffling right through the middle. **Swamp complete!** We

...just till over there!

already had that and not only once.

Once, a creek inmidst the swamp blocks us. About one and a half meters wide and deep up to the thighs. It meanders gladly through the landscape but doesn't offer a single possibility for crossing without efforts and remaining dry.

„Jens, do you remember what we did in a similar situation at the time when we did our second tour?"

„You mean, throwing over?"

I nod and we grab Niklas's backpack. He already jumped over and we instruct him to receive his luggage container properly and take care that it will not roll into the creek after the landing.

Wading in the Willows

As before Jens and I take the backpack between us and swing it to and fro for letting him flow at the command „Three!". But reaching „Two!" we recognize a heavy imbalance, possibly caused by the on top attached moose antler I found some days ago but was not willing to carry. The action is abruptly aborted. The backpack would inevitably hit the creek with a big splash and sink. I'm going to be the martyr and put on my birthday suit from the hips down for carrying the backpacks on the other side one by one. Then I get redressed. And all that for barely 2 meters.

Alas, we are up shit's creek. Quite the opposite: it's going worse. Now we are passing swamp belts, where you sink in deeper that the shoes are high. Water runs in consequently. In plain English: Kneipp cure for the rest of the day. The only thing you have to take care of is, not to scrunch any fish in your shoes.

The physical effort increases consistently and even more with every run-in ascent. We already have abandoned the plan of a stopover. Today's milestone must be Rittak so that we can dry the wet equipment especially the shoes. At the moment, we made the first planned 6 km and I shudder to think of the next six till the vindskydd. At some point the overflowed high plain must come to an end. And then these never ending willows.... That tough and unruly scrub. I'm hag-ridden by that caboodle.

The trees here produce Usnea arborea (Lichen plicatus), which the Laplanders apply to excoriations of the feet caused by excessive walking. They line their shoes with this moss (...). The Laplanders also line their shoes with grass, consisting of various species of Carex, (especially C. sylvatica, Fl. Brit.). This grass they comb with iron or horn combs, bruising it between their hands till it becomes soft and pliable. When dried they cram it into their shoes, and it answers instead of stockings for defending the feet from cold.

[Linné2, pg. 260]

The next long drawn-out ascent stretches my no longer available condition to the limit. I have a feeling that the willow bushes are alive and want me to stay here with might and main. I'm gasping after my comrades, who wait for me on the next rise.

SUCCESS! We are off the willows. „**Swamp complete**" is over. No further bush vegetation to fear. The terrain declines gently in march direction. About 1-2 km ahead, groups of birch trees are visible. The expected treeline is within reach. We assume that after reaching the treeline there will be need only to walk downwards a little through the forest for joining Kungsleden not far from Rittak.

It hasn't been raining up to now. The clouds are still low and cocoon the mountains around. That is the reason evoking disagreement concerning our current location. On the left hand side two cut mountains can be recognized. Niklas's and my opinion is to keep us more easterly, whereas Jens is sure Rittak being in direct line below our current location. We have to pass between the peaks Stuor Dágár and Favnoajvve as we did on the way there. In fact, the low hanging clouds are actually no help for orienting. At least we are convinced by Jens and walk straight-lined in direction of the treeline.

...just till over there!

Full of enthusiasm – as far as some members of this expedition are able to share this feeling – and being of confident hope that we will have made it in foreseeable future, we plunge into pathless birch tree jungle. The number of northern so called „crippled birch trees" is legion. The sub-arctic rain-forest devours us. We are trying to go in straight direction to south, an intention being often torpedoed by the unconventional geological formation. The „precious fall of the folds" in the landscape forces us to make surprising curves and redirections. Very often there are kinds of earth walls that need to be overcome, meaning only a few steep but demanding meters and a strong attack on my last power reserves.

The expected Kungsleden makes itself scarce. Nothing changes concerning this topic. Then Jens is going out of Niklas's and my sight. It is me, who is not able to follow his speed. Well, we will meet him again somewhere.

The Laplanders consult several natural objects by way of compass as they travel.
1. Large Pine-trees, which bear more copious branches on their southern side than towards the north.
2. Ant-hills, the south sides of which bear grass, the northern whortle-berries
3. Aspen trees, whose bark is rough on the north side, smooth on the opposite part.
4. Old withered Pines are clothed, on the north side, with the black Usnea, or filamentous Lichen (L. jubatus).

By such marks as these they are able to find their way through pathless forests. Have we any guides so certain?

[Linné2, pg 171]

In the meanwhile the weather has brightened up. The skies opened and bright sunshine floods the world. Simultaneously it grows significantly warmer and arduous in the woods. We continue stumbling over tree roots and overgrown rocks. After what felt like the 128th geological folding – only 5 m high - I am totally ruined.

„Break, son! I am dead!. I will not do any further step before I know how long it will take to that damned path. That wandering around aimlessly takes away my last quantum power. Let's leave the backpacks here and research the distance from here to the path."

„OK, but how to re-find the bags? We should mark something!"

That is a truly spoken word coming from the mouth of my direct descendant. A mark in thick forest that can be seen from greater distance? Hmmm! I've got an idea.

„We take my red jacket and hang it in a lone tree."

...just till over there!

A word and a blow! It is a bit difficult to hang the jacket on frailed branches in a well-serving high position, while the best reaching branches promptly break, when using them. But finally, we manage it. It is a wonderful feeling walking without crushing weight. Turning around after 50 meters we check the functionality of our signal-tree. It works! Laying on the ground the backpacks have vanished in the thick vegetation. That would have been a funny search operation.

And now follows the big surprise!. After only 200 m we come to cross a narrow beaten track that we clearly identify as a trail. I am very glad about that. The martyrdom of the jungle will only last a few further minutes.

The meanwhile vanished clouds allow a better siting. According to that we did not enter Kungsleden next to Rittak, but **hefty 5 km** away from it. And unfortunately in the wrong direction, namely to the west, heading for Kvikkjokk. We are somewhere in the section between the bridge over the Gallakjåhkå and the mountain Favnoajvve. It was on its top, when we enjoyed the panorama on Tjaktjajaure having just entered the area of Sarek. Now we have to go east. Not only that from the original 6 km became at least expected 12, no, there will be additional 5 km on top. And the next two of them are going to be significantly steep.

Good grief! Actually I would have been already lying in my sleeping bag and rejuvenating. And what next? Niklas leads the way and I follow him doing my very best. I am really exhausted in a way that here and there I am forced to pause and pant for breath every 15-20 m. I give all my hopes in reaching the top of the pass for that the trail will go on horizontally or even descending.

The path is leading between the heights Favnoajvve and Huornnásj. Shortly before reaching the top of the pass we meet Jens again, who finally managed to find Kungsleden, too, and is now waiting for us by the wayside. I am thankful for each break, and for this one, too. There are still 4 km left till Rittak. As the chance of an overcrowded vindskydd is all the more greater the later one will arrive there, it would be wise to move in an expeditious manner. However, this is exactly my current problem.

„You know what?“, I propose, „you both dash ahead and the old man will follow slowly. When you will have arrived and got rid of your luggage one of you will come my way and take at least the tent off my shoulders for the rest of the way.“

They look at each other – do I see something like a sardonic grin on their faces? – nodding their approval. After that they are pushing off. I remain standing, where I am for a few moments before I'm going to drag-ging on at a slow pace. However, it is not as bad as I expected, but never-theless I never could have kept in step with Jens and Niklas in my current physical shape. The prospect of a near end of today's stage seems to in-duce a mentally founded upgrade of my physique.

Indeed, it is going to be significantly more pleasant behind the top of the pass. The ground is becoming increasingly softer and the soil portion on the path greater – compared to the number of stones. Finally, it is a comfortable walking – apart from the damned block on my back. I'm walking slowly but steadily, trying to ignore the pain in my shoulders, what partially succeeds.

Within the tent are spread on each side skins of reindeer, with the hairy part uppermost, on which the people either sit or lie down (...). In the centre of the whole is the fire-place, or a square enclosure of low stones about the ash-heap. (...) In the roof are two racks, suspended over the reindeer skins on each side, upon which cheeses are laid to dry, and before these, towards the entrance, hang rennet-bags, filled with milk, preserved for winter use.

[Linné2, pg 14]

It is about 1 km before Rit-tak, when I see Jens coming my way. He takes the tent and two stuff bags off me. What a relief – in a true literal sense. Now I am able to follow him even in a breakneck speed. As ex-pected the vindskydd is full up so that we are going to stay yet again in the tent. Only 50 m away outside the trees the wet polyester castle will be raised. The weather has remained reasonable during the day, what on the other hand leads to a microclimatic, stuffy zone in our cramped enclave surrounded by green plastic membranes. This state is intensified by the partially wet sleeping bags. Crawling therein is everything but comforta-ble.

But this is the lesser evil. In this sauna like environment some 300 to 400 mosquitos, invaded illegally into the inner tent, feel much more com-fortable than ourselves. It is impossible to squash them all and thus, we are forced to climb down. That means in plain terms: pulling the mosquito nets over the heads for the night and hoping for a few hours of sleep.

Lapland has an extremely varying climate. It may happen that there are minus 30 degrees C for some weeks in the winter, whereas the summer temperature in July regularly is around plus 20 degrees C, sometimes even up to 30 degrees C. The Atlantic climate on the western side of the Scandinavian Range is quite different from the one on the eastern side and in the plateau Lapland. This climatic west-east-divide will strongly be influenced by the Gulf Stream on his far way to north along the Scandinavian west coast. For one thing the winter temperatures will be moderated by the influence of the warm ocean drift, for another thing there will be considerably greater precipitation amounts caused by ascensions of masses of wet air coming from the sea. In contrast the Scandinavian inland is dry, cool and honed by wind at exposed positions and therefore decisively continental influenced. In Finland's Northeast and Norway one may meet typical moors and permafrost soils. Polar climate is present only in the high mountains in the north.

Today's planned 6 km finally turned into 18. We have been 10 hours on the road, going through one or another hell. Now, we are cherishing hopes that a well-intentioned Morpheus will let us slumber in his arms.

It's goodnight, nurse.

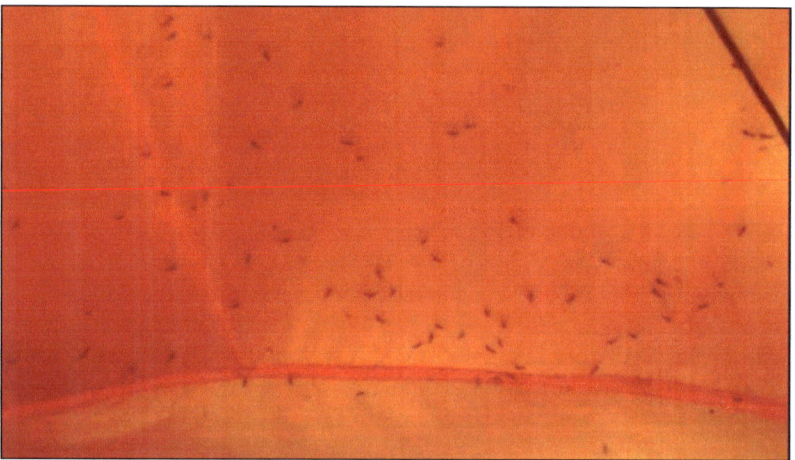

Things could not have been worse...

Day	distance km	meters up + down	start Level	end Level	peaks, rivers, lakes on the way
14	18	700	900	840	Kallakvare (1125 m) Suolanjunnje (1008 m) Favnoaivve (1117 m) Vindskydd Rittak
Cumulated Values	130	7505			

...just till over there!

Day 15 | July, 30th:
Vindskydd Rittak | 5th Rest Day

I didn't sleep well – I'm sore all over! I feel my butt stiff and aching from continuing climbing yesterday. In addition to that thousands of mosquito bites are itching like the devil. It actually doesn't help that it isn't only me suffering from that.

While we are slowly recovering we have breakfast outside the tent before the terrific scenery of Tjaktjajaure. From our beautiful place outside the trees we have a magnificent view on the marvelous panorama the blue lake offers. Nestled in tree-covered borders and with small islands looking like big swimming leaves it simply lies in the sun.

Today there will be no further action, I guess. Yesterday's stage requires a rest. Besides it makes sense to dry all the wet duds. But before doing this it is indicated to slouch in the botany – mosquito-safe wrapped in sleeping bags – and to proceed with a second sleep unit.

Within the trees nearby the vindskydd there is a somewhat greater plane and down-tramped surface that is used by most of the here pausing wanderers as a camping ground. As this has the charm of any old campsite we yesterday decided to settle only 50 m ahead off the woods on thick overgrown soil just 10 m below the path.

The rope we stretched over a few meters between two young birch trees serves as a good laundry line for our wet stuff. Up to now nobody feels like drying the shoes as there are still some people inside the hut. We will wait and see! Seems, it will be sufficiently early after lunch.

The noodle dish is history and Niklas again quarrels with the mosquitos. Indeed, they are really gunning for him. These trunk dudes probably are able to receive such negative, mental vibrations and choose their victims basing thereupon. The knack is sending the message that you didn't give a damn shit, whether those critters are present or not. Alas, Niklas blinds himself to that argumentation and as a result rakes bite for bite in. The areas around both of his elbows are palm-sized reddened. One cannot differentiate between single bites. I can imagine it being totally annoying. But you cannot avoid it by means of mounting anger.

In the meanwhile all the rest of the wanderers are on the road again and left the vindskydd completely. There is a woodstove in the hut and a small timber stock. The plan is to start up the oven and bring the shoes in a suitable distance to the heat for transferring them from wet into dry condition.

The artful appropriation of shoelaces and packing belts lets the clunky kicks be hanging funny on the two metal rods reaching from floor to ceiling on both sides of the oven. We keep a wary eye on the oven and regularly stoke it up with birch tree logs. The temperature inside increases notably. I think we will get a good result, if we put more wood on the fire until we will go to sleep and leave the shoes in the warm hut overnight.

At Rittak above Tjaktjajaure

...just till over there!

Shoeparade in the Rittak Vindskydd

...just till over there!

Day 16 | July, 31ˢᵗ:
Rittak - Aktse

Again lasting rain during the night. Accordingly the morning looks like. Low hanging clouds with little hope for weather improvement.

During a break in the rain we're getting our stuff packed without any rush and get off here shirtsleeved in new drizzle. Must come to an end that bloody rain, sometime!

The path descents over millions of stones until we pass the treeline. In the wood section we sometimes come to cross a swampy passage. As we are on a „maintained" trail such stretches of way are protected by wooden paths. Now and then the double balance beam is torn into pieces. As we can see it here: over a length of 20 m or 4 to 5 plank lengths the wood path is broken. The planks are lying around unfixed partially without any substruction directly on the ground and badly laid next to each other. Usually you will find not less than 2 of these 10-cm-wide planks in parallel.

What does not apply in the present case. One has to balance on single, sometimes wobbling planks and should not dream or chasing mosquitos while doing so.

Niklas walks between Jens and me. On a rather fixed plank surrounded by moisture he suddenly slips, steps with his left foot besides the wood on supposed solid soil and bogs down in the mud up to the thigh. The trouble is that it is quite difficult to get out of such a situation on your own without dirtying up yourself anymore. Fortunately, Jens is only a few steps away that he can pull Niklas back on dry land.

The next kilometers leading us through forest until Laitaure were rather eventless except the permanent mosquito attacks. Reaching the lake we instantly recognize only 1 boat lying on the bank. That means a triple rowing course over the water. Alas, there is nobody coming from the opposite direction during our preparations for taking off. At least each of us rows a complete distance. After all, the weather remained stable since we plunged into the forest.

We actually wanted to make only the last kilometer till the station of Aktse and raise the tent in its environment. And to pick provisions in form of only saving „Köttbullars". They are available in the shop there.

However, STF's new pricing policy confounds that plan radically. The stugvard (responsible person for the station during the season) seriously requires 200,- SKR (Swedish Crowns) **per capita** for clearing a piece of wild, waist-high covered meadow by your own and raising your tent there. There is NO fee for the tent!

„200 crowns per person, yes, <u>but the tent is free!</u>" Seldomly laughed as much.

200 crowns are somewhat like 25 Euros – and now take it thrice! It would be okay once for the tent, but per capita with a simple garden shower connected to the on-site glacial stream as the only bought comfort is unacceptable. We do not defer to that and at least go to climb the next very steep meters in height till the road junction above the treeline. Here, a path branches off leading on top of the Skierffe.

We purchase the obligatory Köttbullar for supper in the provisions shop and get off. Contrary to our expectations the ascent is not that eerie. Even myself is heaving up steadily and sooner as expected we reach the junction.

In the light of the descending, but not completely disappearing midnight sun we have a marvelous

> *I could not observe that the nights were at all less light than the days, except when the sun was clouded.*
>
> *[Linné1, pg. 157]*

view on the lake Laitaure and the mountain Tjahkelij opposite to us. We deign us this panorama only for a short moment, because in this moment priority one is to building up the tent and getting up SUPPER.

Mmmh, mashed potatoes and plenty of Köttbullar. We soak up this „Last Supper" suitable for geriatric means appreciatively, toss down another two teas and give ourselves successfully to lassitude.

Day	distance km	meters up + down	start Level	end Level	peaks, rivers, lakes on the way
16	13	630	840	780	Laitaure (rowing 3 km) Nammatj (823 m) Skierffe (1079 m) Aktse Fjällstation Junction for Skierffe
Cumulated Values	143	8135			

...just till over there!

Day 17 | August, 1st:
Aktse - beyond Sitojaure

I awake early in the morning. Bladder pressure keeps me on the move into the cool of the early morning. The glowing ball in the sky is slowly raising over the mountains and with a single lonely trickling spurt I'm staring into the clear distance. Laitaure lies still beyond me. There is not the slightest breath of wind that could get its surface in motion. Tjahkelij's mirror image punctuated with small, tree-covered islets in the lake. The foot of the mountain still shows rests of morning clouds sticking thereon. I am surrounded by perfect silence.

I'm hastening back to the tent for fetching my camera and making pictures of these wonderful moments. Being well dressed against the morning chill with panties, undershirt and sandals I climb the next hill and capture the quiet Laitaure on celluloid.

The sun is going up gently timidly illuminating the mountainside of Tjahkelij and the Nammatj – enthroned in the Rapa delta. Halfway thereto the remarkable Skierffe stretches up its 700-m-steep-face into the early-morning sky. Jens and I were on the top of Skierffe, when we did our first common Lapland-tour and enjoyed the marvelous view on the Rapa delta below us.

I'm going back to lie down again – the two figures besides me haven't moved a single inch. Indeed, I fall asleep once again.

Rain wakes me up. A look outside shows nothing more than clouds and fog. The rain is varying and reaches from slight drizzle, over drizzle in squally winds up to clattering big raindrops. Additionally: without any prospect of an end. The clear weather situation we had in the morning couldn't catch on.

Herewith, the vaguely planned side trip on the Skierffe is history. A 4 -5 hours march (to and fro) for an expected view of zero isn't a worthwile thing. Thus, we start in drizzling rain after having packed the backpacks uncomfortably inside the tent.

Despite the threatening dark clouds above the rain stops after a short while. And so it remains.

Firstly, it goes up a bit and then over the high plain we already crossed a fortnite ago till the descent into the next valley, in which the lake Sitojaure lies. The forest belt spreads over more than 2 kilometers up to the lake.

When we reach the lakeside a motorboat is just leaving, carrying rowing-shy wanderers to the other side. Now, the landing stage reaching a few meters into the water will be orphaned for a while.

...just till over there!

Landing Stage at Sitojaure

On this lakeside there is a vindskydd, too. When we were here the first time some days ago, we built up a little depot under the hut, which was built on small rocks as foundation. We are going to check it immediately and realize that is has been untouched. There is at least one "normal" bar of chocolate for Jens and me. We already finished with the rest of them and Niklas has let us participate in his special lactose-free (-L) chocolate during the last days.

The weather has become significantly better. Actually the sun is breaking through the cloudy sky.

„Well, let's go for lunch", Jens says, „preferably on the landing stage. It's dry over there".

No sooner said than done! Fishing out stove and raw materials for a spicy noodle dish, instantly. There's a decisive amount of provisions still available. It is the same regarding the ever-present hunger. Thus, we prepare a large portion of pasta and dine as the ancient Romans in decumbence. At those times they would have call it "orgy". The only thing we have to take care of is to avoid the cutlery falling between the cracks of the planks.

...just till over there!

Bathing Fun in Sitojaure

„What about a plunge into the lake and washing off the sweat", Jens says. „I guess I'll go for a bath".

A scrutinizing look into the skies promises continuing half-sunny atmosphere. Best conditions for a suitable bathing session.

L'etat lapone – c'est moi!

...just till over there!

The landing stage becomes an undressing area and promptly we are dabbling in the cool, but refreshing water. This feeling of relationship with nature you get during such actions is indescribable. At least you are wading into natural waters far away from any civilization and being enclosed by „wild waters“. Of course, the water is quite cold, but you will adapt to it after a while, and if you were once dived completely it is simply fantastic. Our wet bodies are drying in the mild wind with thick white clouds above.

We rest for a spell – no stress at all – as we have to row soon. The good news is that here again 2 boats are waiting for us. That means that there is need to pass the 4 km rowing course only once. On the other side the landing stage is located in the environment to Sitojaurestugorna, the STF station at Sitojaure. As we do not feel like marching on after the rowing, we think about setting up the camp near the station.

Niklas and Jens take it in turns to row. Restraining myself I keep the others sailing me lordly over the gentle waves. It's a good thing having some people for the rough jobs.

On Sitojaure

The camping ground on the other bank is quasi directly besides the landing stage. A handwritten note tells everyone – who actually does not want to know it – that here again the 200-crowns-rule for spending the night in a tent is valid, too. Seems the slogan „tent free“ is obligatory predefined by the headquarters of STF. Well, they are welcome to frame it. Somewhere a limit is achieved, when it turns into daylight robbery.

We will not support this strange policy. The backpacks are strapped on and dandling through the forest belt for another hour. Only one kilometer ahead we find a nice place. Nearly rocks-free, slightly covered with low juniper plants and therefore it is a soft lying surface. We've got a nice view on the lake, where the rowing course can easily be traced back.

We manage to raise the tent very quickly. It may get dry in the warm sun. While Jens is drawing a further noodle dish to completion, Niklas and I are collecting branches and trash the wind has broken from solitary trees. We pick small strings of typical parchment-like bark of birch trees and prepare to start a fire.

With intent not to destroy the vegetation cover by burning, we cut out a rectangle piece of the ground, roll up the vegetation cover and place the fire pit on the naked earth. There is still salami in supply that needs urgently to be charred. As a dessert, of course.

We are feasting like the kings.

„What's about our provisions?" Jens asks between two spoons pasta al dente.

„There's enough for main meals for the remaining days. Don't know how much muesli – I have nothing more. Niklas, what about you?"

It turns out that there is plenty of muesli left. Seems, during the last two weeks the chef de cuisine was using it extremely sparingly. The result is we can triple the muesli ration easily during the coming days. It would have been better, if we had done inventory in between and increased the rations earlier.

The warm temperatures invite to drape all the wet or moisty stuff in the botany. A new laundry line will be installed and a big rock hosts willingly our complete shoe equipment lying on their sides and turned towards the wind. The full moon appearing on the actually not dark sky looks down on an entirely full and satisfied combo. Terrific!

Day	distance km	meters up + down	start Level	end Level	peaks, rivers, lakes on the way
17	7	500	780	660	Rengärde Kablajaure (rowing 4 km) Sitojaurestugorna Fjällstation
Cumulated Values	150	8635			

...just till over there!

Day 18 | August, 2nd:
Sitojaure till Vindskydd Autsutjvagge

I make a short trip under a clear sky in the night. The full moon is glowing over the silhouettes of the mountain ridges. It is cold. After having done my business I return into the tent quickly. Niklas pesters me in his sleep with his camping mat so that I can hardly move.

I wake up in the morning. It is awfully warm inside the tent. The blazing sun beats down on the polyester. Due to the mosquitos I was wearing a shirt during the night. Now, I can't stand it any longer being inside. I need fresh air. I dress completely and go for fresh water. Therefore it is said to walk about 500 meters to the small creek we crossed yesterday while coming up from the lake. Alas, the mosquitos are awake, too. It is pesky having buzzing sputniks round the head all the time, while filling the bottles and water bag.

Yesterday's inventory unveiled that there are indeed 4 packs of muesli left. The resulting triple ration is taken outside in the sunshine sitting on the camping mats. Afterwards we are dozing with the skulls in mosquito nets and the rest of the body well packed in sleeping bags. You can't walk on a full stomach.

Somewhen a dark cloud is sailing in. We are afraid that the now dried tent will be soaking wet again and pack up leisurely.

During the act of packing 4 friendly greeting wanderers pass by not without admiring our 20-m-laundry line. The fireplace will carefully be renaturated; all other marks of our "being here" airbrushed. Each snippet will be collected and put into the trash bag.

Finally, there was no rain! We leave this beautiful place at noon. The path goes up for some easygoing 70 meters in height with different kinds of ground until we reach the 800-m-mark. Sometimes the path is stony, sometimes soft or even mixed. After 2 km an

> *A cheer, you men and beasts and birds, for the lonely night in the woods, the woods! A cheer for the darkness and God's murmur between the trees, for the sweet and simple melodious sound of silence in my ears, for the green leaves and the yellow leaves! A cheer for the sound of life I hear.*
>
> *[Hamsun, pg. 942]*

apparently derelicted reindeer corral appears on the left hand side below the mountain Tjirák.

The path winds along the stretched mountainside of Tjiráksnjunnje over dozens of small humps. A handful of brooks come down the heights and confluence in the Avtsusjjåhkå, which feeds the lake Pietsaure some 15 km ahead. Roughly 2 km before reaching today's stage, the vindskydd Autsutjvagge, a nearly equally long and pretty valley opens with the Avtsusjjåhkå right in the middle of it. We do not descent into the valley, but follow the path along its upper edge.

After having covered a distance of 10 km in short of 3 hours we finally reach the destination. There were some brief encounters en route – remember that we are on Kungsleden – nevertheless, the lodging is fortunately empty. There is a low probability of occurring that somebody else will join us today. Due to that we decide to move into the shelter instead of tenting, although using the vindskydd for this purpose is usually reserved for emergency cases. Well, let me say it this way: 3 days ago our tent suffers a rip in the outer skin - impressive 10 cm long, which is sufficient for justification.

In return we are going to knock the shack into German shape. Giving the floor a perfect sweep – even in the corners and under the benches – collecting obvious garbage in a bag and making some firewood for the iron stove from some old planks lying around.

After work is done we enjoy spaghetti with chili sauce. The mosquito population is within limits here, so that we take the meal outside on the "front porch". During the slow walk in the near area afterwards we collect further dry wood for burning. In fact, I manage to get the fire starting and warm tea perfects the homelike mood.

As he did quite often in the recent days, the Saxon again abruptly knocks out one of his ideas.

„Gosh! Look at those hot stones on the stove. If we only could dash some mint or something similar on them."

„But we do have OLBAS!", it sounds in unison from father and son. (OLBAS is a Chinese medicine in form of drops that heals everything). The China stuff is pulled out quickly and seconds later we pour the drops over the heated rocks. Not bad, I admit; irritates the eyes a bit but it's okay.

In the meanwhile a young couple has arrived in the area of the hut, now looking for a proper camp ground. In fact there are so many one simply should choose the next one. There are dozens of flat areas on soft ground. We are dealing with the question to go over and collect 200 crowns per capita.

...just till over there!

Vindskydd Autsutjvagge

A small window with a size of about 40x50 cm is mounted inside the door. Like grannies in the German Ruhr-Area we are stuck to the pane and flatten our noses while observing the two people. They scurry from pillar to post, then vanish behind a small elevation and do s o m e t h i n g at the little pond. What they are doing exactly is beyond our knowledge, but we recognize slight undulation in the water coming obviously from that blind angle.

There occur further waves for quite a while but nothing else happens. None of the two heroes is to be seen. Thus, this broadcaster becomes boring and we switch it off.

Being embedded more or less comfortable on those hard wooden pallets we are trying to drop off to sleep.

Day	distance km	meters up + down	start Level	end Level	peaks, rivers, lakes on the way
18	10	20	660	640	Autsutjvagge Vindskydd Autsutjvagge
Cumulated Values	160	8655			

...just till over there!

Day 19 | August, 3rd:
Vindskydd Autsutjvagge till Saltoluokta

The plank beds are really hard as stone and despite of air matresses inconvenient. They are probably too equable without any stoops or hollows, in which you can fit the one or other body roundings. Thus, we are accordingly tired, when we start the breakfast. Of course we have a huge portion of muesli – the stuff has to be used up anyway. In the aftermath the hut is going to be undergone a final cleaning of the kind: deeply German.

There are only 9 kilometers to go on this journey. There is a silent melancholy around us when we get started to the final stage. Halfway to Saltoluokta, we want to pick up Jens's trolley we have deposited somewhere in the bushes. We kept the place in mind so it should be easy to rediscover it.

Reaching the place lateron we found it empty. We scour the near surrounding in case we are wrong. But the search result remains negative. We are at a loss with this situation, until Jens discovers the drawbar leaning vertically against a big rock – some 100 meters away.

While getting closer to it we notice that something is wrong. Somebody found the trolley, broke off the „baggage rack" with the wheel forcefully and – *stole* it. I have never considered something like that possible and now it happened. A wanderer steals from a like-minded one. Up to this moment I would have vouched for the impossibleness of such an act – especially here in the northern wilderness – and I am sad about that.

Usually the rule is: what is not mine, remains not mine. And to make matters worse, Jens didn't fling the thing wildly into the landscape, but put it neatly on a well-chosen place. The kind of deposition showed clearly, that the owner would return. The tarp all parts were wrapped with is missing, too, and if the harness weren't screwed tight to the drawbar, it would be gone, either. This is an example for an aggravated theft. My confidence is devastated and I try to persuade myself that we witnessed an isolated case the „mass tourism" on Kungsleden has brought along. Obviously, there are subjects on the road with an obscure mental orientation.

Jens cannot believe it. It makes him so angry that he is burning up with anger and weighing 4 quintals for fury. We are sprawling out and sifting through the bushes by the wayside for at least 500 meters in each direction, hoping that the stolen goods became a burden to the thief and he finally threw them away. Alas, we do not find anything.

...just till over there!

Jens disassembles the remaining parts of the trolley completely that only the two drawbars stay over. At least the harness should be worth saving. We don't like to leave the drawbars in the fjäll, but want to get rid of them in Gällivare later.

I minimize my hiking sticks and use the drawbars instead. If somebody should ask for them I will argue that I'm walking with „High Mountain Sticks – new ergonomic line". Well, there was actually nobody who asked directly, but quizzical looks were already present.

High Mountain Sticks

We are marching swiftly through to Saltoluokta. Before re-entering the woods we have a wonderful view on the lake Langas, lying deeply blue at our feet, framed by the mountains Lulep Gierkav on the southern side and the Juobmotjåhkkå on the northern side.

Jens is nourishing the hope to get hold of the bloody thief in Salto and therefore quickens his paces instinctively. But the odds are long, because

...just till over there!

firstly we do not know, which day the theft was committed and secondly it is unsure whether the thief was on the way to Salto.

Well, although we range over the Saltoluokta area with eager eyes directly after we arrived there, scanning every backpack we see for Jens's spokewheel, there is no success in this affair. It's better that way, I guess. I have no idea what should have happened, if Jens got hold of the bastard.

The station is well-filled. No wonder in the main season. All beds – and after all there are 100 at disposal – seem to be filled. The shop in the station is open and so we allow ourselves cookies, Cola and soda.

Here again a night stop in the tent costs 200 crowns per capita – within the fee required zone. Outside the "many-crowns-zone" it's free and here are many nice places. We choose one at the end of a gravel path only 30 meters away from the lakeside and simultaneously in just 200 meters distance to the main building of the station.

Once all is arranged well, we (again) have a refreshing bath in the lake. The warm sunshine feels pleasantly on the naked skin. This kind of bathing is simply incomparable.

We ease into the next steps – we've made it at least. The last stage has beeb walked, the weather is fantastic and the day isn't out yet.

We collect wood in the near surrounding and start a fire at the given fire place next to our tent. The second last salami has to go west. Like several times before the slices are burnt over open fire. Then all will be washed down with a sumptuous Asia noodle dish.

At the end of the day we are going to visit the old Sami church hut, the kirkkotan, in the nearby village, which is nowadays changed into a market place for Sami handicraft. Niklas is enthusiastic about the rustic building, a wooden construction covered with earth and grass sods. A rough entrance of birch trunks invites to approach, while the crooked flue seems to grow out of a mound of earth. The floor inside is completely covered with leafy birch twigs shedding fragrance all over.

You will find little goods here, crafted by Laplanders living in the wider area around Saltoluokta, such as the classic bracelets made of braided tin wire combined with reindeer leather. Or complete huge reindeer antlers and fur or small seat pads from reindeer fur for the beloved ones at home.

We end the day in the entrance hall of the ancient 100-years-old STF-station. It is one of the first stations being raised by the young association „Svenska Turist Föreningen". Three armchairs stand directly in front of an open-hearth fireplace. We settle down here, even if the fireplace is not in operation at the moment due to the warm weather.

The other guests have been retired to their accomodations (tent or room). We are going to do the same, but not without setting the alarm clock for 0715, because starting from 0730 you may have Frokost (breakfast) in the great Matsal (dining room).

We do not want to miss that.

Former Sapmi Church Hut near Saltoluokta

Final score after 19 days:

Day	distance km	meters up + down	start Level	end Level	peaks, rivers, lakes on the way
19	9	265	640	375	Saltoluokta Fjällstation
Cumulated Values	**169**	**8920**	Total (plus 14 km rowing!)		

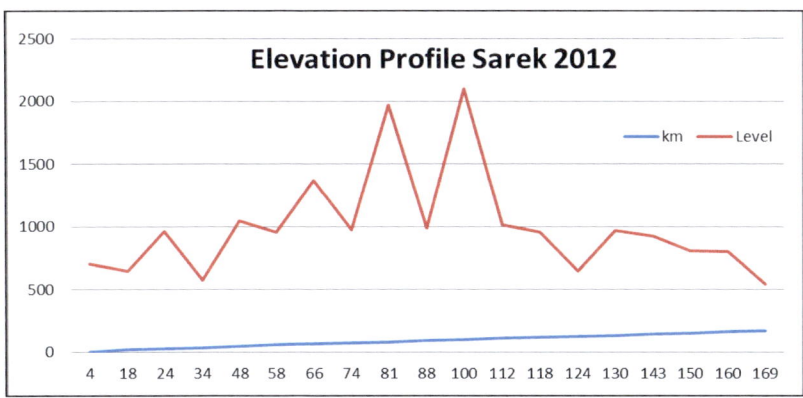

...just till over there!

Saturday, August, 4th:
Departure

The prospect of solid food for breakfast does not make us stay longer than necessary in the sleeping bags. The entrance hall is already filled with hungry people, waiting for admission to the **Matsal**.

Dining Room in Saltoluokta

We enter a nice, bright and rustic room with many windows, to which great tables with 8 seats were established. The first half of the room comes up with a great oval wooden table offering a buffet. Diverse kinds of bread, cold cuts, cheese, eggs, cucumber, tomatoes, paprika – much less muesli, gruel, rice pudding and berries.

In addition to that they serve COFFEE - hot, strong, tasty and much of it. We eat until the navel shines. Alas, it doesn't take long until we reach this state because during the last three weeks we have been weaned from solid food that we soon have had enough. Nevertheless, we enjoy the wonderful atmosphere among all those hungry wanderers.

There is plenty of time left till the ferry M/S Langas will cross over to Kebnats. Thus, we indulge in cloudless blue skies and comfortable temperatures, sitting at a table outside and watching the people, some of which are preparing for departure, too.

The boat is full to the brim. A pile of backpacks is decked up in the bow. And there will be more, so that parts of the load has to be packed on the roof of the cabin.

It is the same concerning the bus. It arrives in time but is already well filled. Including the new passengers from the boat, the bus is full to the last seat. A problem occurs while trying to pay the fare. As we calculated on the possibility to pay with plastic money in long-distance buses we only have a small amount of cash. This is usually no problem, but today of all days the credit card reader in this very bus is out of order. No mon, no fun, as the folk saying goes. But the warm hearted bus captain will take us along under the condition to draw some bucks from a cash machine in Gällivare.

There is fine weather throughout the journey giving the chance of nice views into the nature. Thus, amongst others we pass Sjaunja- and Muddus Nationalpark. Somewhere on the way a reindeer is trotting over the lane. It looks old and the worse for wear with its tattered hide. This is our 4th reindeer that we've come to see during the last 3 weeks. And we met them all on the highway, none in the fjäll. I have never experienced anything like this. What a pity!

Reaching Gällivare we take care of the affair with the bus captain and adjourn promptly to the campsite for moving into the reserved hut, where we get off the baggage and go for the next open supermarket immediately. We are hungry and here you can get all you need for a feast: noodles, 4 cans of köttbullar, 1 can of ice cream, cranberries, cookies, potatoe chips and beverages.

Just back in the hut an act of meaningless gluttony is being put in execution as well skilled as intense. In the end we can hardly move. Those, who have any physical capacities left, yomp to the shower while the rest of us stares with unseeing eyes into the Swedish telly.

At least we enter the bunks for spending the last night on Lappish ground north of the Arctic Circle.

I lie in the top bunk recalling the recent weeks in my mind's eye. How nice it was.

Even, if we couldn't do the originally planned route. There were lots of experiences and landscapes. As for me for one thing, I am really pleased that my junior is as keen as mustard, too, and for another thing that there were absolutely no disagreements between us three expedition participants. Niklas has fit into our little group in an outstanding way being an emancipated member from the start. He took over tasks eagerly and on his own initiative equally to Jens and me.

I got the best endorsement for having done this journey some 10 days after our return, when Niklas had finished another camping tour he made with some of his friends in the Ruhr Area in our home pastures, being scarcely back from the North.

He literally said: „You know what, dad? Camping on a caravan site – that is blowing goats!"

There is nothing left to be added.

...just till over there!

I (a

le

af

fa

ll

s)

one

l

iness

[--e.e.cummings]

How I respect
the old Sámi life
That was true love of nature
where nothing was wasted
where humans were part of nature
Our ancestors have made a fire
on every slope
they have stepped on
every stone
our ancestors
they have lived and died here
(...)
How I respect old Sápmi
How could they have lived for
then thousand years
without the right
to call the Sámiland Sápmi
without the right to Sápmi
to be Sámi

How can I explain
that I cannot live in just one place
and still live
when I live
among all these tundras
You are standing in my bed
my privy is behind the bushes
the sun is my lamp
the lake my wash bowl
How can I explain
that my heart is my home
that it moves with me
(...)
Fly beyond Thoughts
The redness of evening
Birch tops sway against the sky
The reflection of light in the river
Everything remains unsaid
Still
[Valkeapää2]

...just till over there!

Tips for Beginners

Please find below some tips for trekking beginners, which deal as well with general topics as with specific ones. All of them derive from own experiences.

Hope, they will be a help for a successful tour.

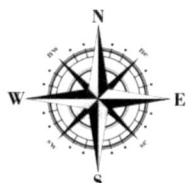

The most unpleasant component for being in the lucky mood to wander within the Promised Land at all is finally to reach it. Usually we speak about average distances of about 2.500 km for trekking candidates, whose central living point is in Germany.

Tip: Arrival

Basically there are 3 possible jars of transport the wanderer can use: car, train and plane.

Those, who want to travel by **car**, should care about the long distance and think about how much time (and energy) should be wasted for both the way to and fro. German trekkers must accept between 2.300 and 3.000 km for ONE turn — dependent on the federal state they live in (e.g.: Munich-Gällivare = 2.800 km; Flensburg-Gällivare=2.100 km)! Bochum-Gällivare=2.500 km, which means in total **4 days** with 11 driving hours per day at a velocity of 120 km/h. In addition to that the average costs for fuel (imagine a consumption 7 l/100 km and 1,60 EUR/l) will be ca. **560 EUR** completely.

Taking the **train** is much more convenient. When I travelled by train in former days it took about 36 hours (Bochum-Abisko) and I think the fee for train tickets being cheaper than the fuel. You should spend a good deal of time asking Aunt Google for price reductions in all going-through countries (e.g. Scan rail-Ticket in Sweden). Total expenditure of time in this case: **72 hours**.

Regarding only the time to spent, the **plane** is unbeatable. In the current case the travel time from departing Düsseldorf till arriving in Gällivare was about 8 h plus 1,5 hours checking in. That is in total a little less than **20 hours** at a price of ca. **450 EUR** there and back. Here too, it is recommended to go through the internet.

...just till over there!

Now, there are indeed people, who want to celebrate their (trek-king)premiere into unknown territories blue-eyed with a simultaneously missing of any experience in this affair and wondering about „suddenly" occurring bad situations causing possibly severe problems.

You will find some "milestones" for planning below, that should be present just by using the common sense.

Tip: Planning

- determine the **target area.**

- get a **hiking map** of the target area; the best for Swedish Lapland is called - **Nya Fjäll-kartan** on a scale of 1:100.000, sheets BD01 to BD10; for Norway choose **Turkart** on a scale of 1:100.000 or 1:50.000 – depending on the region; for Finland **Retkeilyopas & Kartta** on a scale of 1:100.000 or 1:50.000 – depending on the region.

- choose your **route** and herewith take care of...

- ...the **time budget** and the **own physical constitution**.

- include **extra days**, when you do not want to walk due to bad weather, exhaustion, breaks or whatever. Do not forget to consider time for arrival and departure.

- choose a **marked/signed path,** if you want to use the advantages of mountain stations (overnight staying; food), which affects directly on the weight of your backpack. There are lots of information about those stations in the internet.

- choosing a route **cross-country** calculate the needed food. There is a rule of thumb, say-ing: 1 kg per person and day (= sumptuous); this can be taken for short tours (up to 7 days), for greater distances calculate with max. 500-600 g per person and day.

- look for difficult passages, while **studying the map**. Contour lines being close together mean steep passages in natural life.

- check your **equipment** timely. Missing parts should be got in time. The most important things are good shoes, good backpack and a good tent.

- calculate on **bad weather**. Carry gloves and skull cap with you – even in the summer.

...just till over there!

A real diehard couchpotatoe would never choose a holiday trip as it is described in this book. That is presumably because of the minor supply of battery driven TV sets and the hardly manageable volume of a 3-week-stock of potatoe chips and flips and saltsticks. Not to mention the beer in this context.

But even those, who are not members of this fringe group and do sporting activities regularly, should keep a critical eye on their own fitness. Bear in mind that a constant physical stress comes up and at the latest after two days one will apperceive parts of the body, their existence was not known before.

The bottom line is: who is sitting in a warm farted armchair today and wants to slave away the full to bursting backpack cross the landscape the day after tomorrow, is actually in a bad starting position. Therefore it is a good idea, to adopt preventive actions.

Tip: Physical Preparation

For people like me, who do not really much sports during the year and are nothing more than desk criminals, a targeted physical preparation is recommended. The necessity for that increases proportional to the final weight of the backpack. Regarding a 3-week-tour without any options to get food and forced to drag tent, cooker, sleeping bag and all the other junk along, you will end (for 2 persons) not less than 30 kg per head. That's no small affair, that you will not cut it the way: away-from-desk-and-off-into-the-wilderness. Unless you like to be laid low with a totally lame body at the end of the first stage.

My experiences are, that at least during the last 6 weeks before leaving regular familiarizing periods for legs, back and neck will make the first days of the trek considerably bearable than without these actions. Do it by walking with your backpack with some weight in it (sandbags, bell weights....) for one or two hours per action.

Depending on how the terrain you want to cruise is designed, a good exercise to train gradients is simply by climbing stairs. Buildings with a considerable number of floors are predestinated for this purpose. The G-buildings of the Ruhr-University in Bochum offer a dozen floors. You know what you have done, if you climbed sometimes "from the cellar to the roof".

Those, who think this stupid should accept: *learn to suffer without moaning.*

...just till over there!

Making a tour on the marked paths of the northern hiking clubs STF (Svenska Turistföreningen) and DNT (Den Norske Turistföreningen), one has at least once the chance to buy food in one of the stations along. Otherwise, on beforehand, the complete need of food must be procured, prepared for the trek and deported to the starting point. The quantity depends on the length of the tour, the kind of food on the individual favorable preferences.

On storing the nosh away, you should take care of leakproof envelopments and – if possible – of decreasing the volume.

Tip: Procuring Provisions

So-called outdoor nourishment (quite often titled with survival food) compared to conventional supermarket packet soups and the like presents anyhow the "advantage" of higher prices, but not necessarily more ingredients.

In my opinion the discounter option is a very good alternative for victualing. That means, get into the supermarkets and buy packet soups and ready-meals (all of them dehydrated, of course). Make a list, on which days what dish shall be served, that you will buy

a) the correct total quantity and

b) the right number of similar dishes, if more than one item shall be prepared simultaneously.

Item b) can be disregarded, if you don't give it a toss, cooking broccoli-cream-soup and oxtail soup together and it's all right as long as the cup is full up.

Tip: Jazzing up Provisions

Besides muesli, instant soups and other kinds of dry food **salamis** (recommended size: 750 g – that are regularly 35-cm-big-size-sausages with a serious diameter) offer a highly welcome variation in the diet. In this case there is at least something to chew on from time to time.

In the open fire charred slices of salami are an exquisite highlight. Spitted on small twigs – if you are able to find some in the fjäll – or on the ends of small reindeer antlers and held in the flames, the mouth is watering while observing how the fat drops hissing into the fire and the slices bow appetizingly in the heat.

Marvelous!

...just till over there!

Tip: Collocation of Provisions

The main question concerning the food results is bound to occur from chosen route; i.e. is it possible to have a second helping during the tour or not. In the first case the decisive advantage is on one hand a significantly lower weight on the back and on the other hand the great freedom to choose nourishment despite their dosage form (heavy canned food or glass envelopments) or nutrient values.

If you are forced to heft the food for the complete tour from the beginning, you should keep a keen eye on the nutrient values in combination with the weight and volume by collocating the provisions. Avoid heavy (glass) and bulky packages.

Read an extract from our foodlist here:

- breakfast:
  muesli, **skimmed milk powder** (dissolves in water better than whole milk powder), 2 packages **FinnCrisp** (crisp bread) for the first days on tour, **honey** (in a plastic squeeze bottle — saving pains in transferring the sticky stuff from a glass into a light plastic case), **nutnougat cream** for the connoisseurs of us.

- dinner:
  spaghetti, **potatoe dishes** (half-done; e.g. roast potatoes, rösti), dehydrated **noodle dishes** and **soups**, solid nourishment in form of **salamis** (750-g-sticks with an average diameter of 6-7 cm).

- inbetween-meals:
  mueslibars, chocolate, nuts, raisins, vitamin-mineral-tablets, tea, dried fruit.

Watch your individual hunger limit when calculating the quantities. As a rule of thumb it is: 1 kg per person and day — but I think it bases on old-fashioned availabilities, when dehydrated ready meals were not as in wide use as nowadays. We planned 35 kg food for 3 persons and 3 weeks; that is approximately about 600 g per person and day.

It should be clear to everyone, that a tour without any possibility to regain food is far away from being a gourmet tour.

Tip: Packing Provisions

As a general rule the provisions' volume should be minimized. Take care, that the internal space of your backpack will not be queered by unconsolidated milk powder or muesli or the like. Especially the crystal clear muesli envelopments tend to destroy themselves willingly and quickly

Therefore it is worthwhile spending some time on repacking the unconsolidated stuff into convenient units. 3-l-freezer bags are eminently qualified for this purpose. You can gain additional assurance (against leaking and getting dampish) by putting each filled bag into a second one.

...just till over there!

Tip: Compress Provisions

A small pack size is principal duty. Nourishment bags with dehydrated content can mar-velously be compressed. Simply pierce a hole through the upper part of the bag and roll it up tightly from the bottom end for pressing out the containing air. A piece of Scotch tape around it — the small soup role is ready. Similar dishes can be stuck together — saves painful searching in the dark backpack. Don't forget to label the role, because it might be difficult to recognize the content in the coiled state.

Tip: Send Provisions Ahead

The other side of the coin of 3 weeks freedom and solitude are the necessarily enormous logistics. Being outdoor for 20 days means a payload not less than 35 kg per person. This tonnage needs to be deported into the target area.

Dependent on the chosen transport mode this part of the journey might develop more or less strength-sapping and is possibly cost-intensive.

The opportunity arises to get the uncomplicated Swedish guys and their friendliness on board. This way I sent to banana boxes stuffed with provisions by mail to Saltoluokta, where they were stored in the cellar there until our arrival.

...just till over there!

„Who puts himself in danger, will lose his life!". One could say so. But it does not have to. One can gird oneself against a lot of things and requisition relevant quack remedies from the fund of your local drugstore.

Tip: Medicines

It is worth it to carry a backpack-size pharmacy with you on longer trekking tours and other outdoor activities.

That becomes all the more important with increasing distance to the nearest medical care. The backpack-pharmacy should be adapted to the planned length of the tour and the area you want to walk in.

The basic equipment should contain in any case disinfectant and alcohol pads, plaster, different kinds of dressing material, painkillers as well as ointment, elastic bandages, cold medicine, medicine against diarrhea/constipation, antispasmodic agents. In addition to that accessories as space blanket, sterile gloves, a pair of pincers and tick forceps should not be missed. Ditto a signaler like a flare gun or a mirror.

Due to a long term operational capability, the backpack-pharmacy must be waterproof packed, for not becoming unusable by thunderstorms or other flooding incidents.

Many well-known outfitters supply outdoor **First-Aid-Kits,** which are a good basis.

Presumably, everyone would mention other things, if it has to do with the naming of helpful things. Personally, I would take a rope with me in any case, because it can be used in many situations and can simplify many a thing.

Tip: Rope

I detected that a rope can be a useful utensil, even if you take it only as a laundry line for drying your wet stuff. Or for rappelling the backpack in a difficult passage. Or, or, or...

20 – 30 meters rope from an outdoor shop (thickness 5 mm is enough) may work miracles and have no great weight.

...just till over there!

Even having broken in a pair of shoes is no guarantee for blister-free feet inmidst or at the end of a tour. But you can get there by means of targeted measures. Even the worst case scenario - an open, weeping, deep blister – is successfully treatable in that way, that the leftover part of the tour passes off free from pain.

Tip: Prophylactic Measures against Blisters – Toes/Heel

Getting problems with „irritated" little toes in his shoes after several hours walking, one can avoid this easily with a simple prophylaxis.

Get some thin (2 – 3 mm) foam material, cut a 15 cm strip and wrap it freely round your toes. Start between the big toe and its neighbour, pull the strip between all toes finally wrap the little, outer toe and return the strip the same way back. Hereby the foam will not get out of place while walking.

A good source for thin foam material are fruit-boxes. Look for it in super markets or on weekly markets. Otherwise contact a drapery shop.

The classic region for getting blisters, the heel, can be protected easily **on beforehand** by means of **broad leucoplast (5 cm).** Once taped round the heel it works miracles.

Of course, this measurement can be adopted for all other individual weak spots. The silk version with plain surface is no good option in my opinion, because the stuff does not adhere to the skin properly.

For special cases, when an open blister needs to be treated medically *see tip: Treatment of Blisters.*

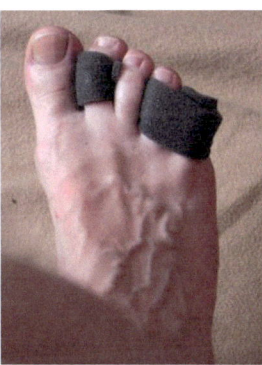 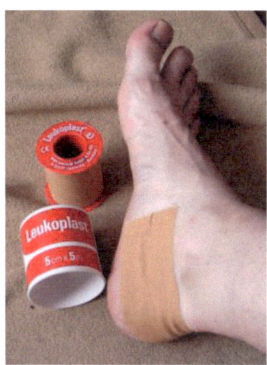

Tip: Treatment of Blisters

For one reason or the other a blister has appeared, is more or less painful and is no real pleasure to walk with. The following description works provably. *(The raw meat in the first picture is my own heel as it surprised me in the evening of the second day on tour in Lapland in 2000, when I detected a bit too late, that the stuffing of my inner shoe was defect.)*

When it has come so far (and I think all previous steps in the lifecycle of a blister can be treated the same way) act as follows:

(1) The first is to keep the tissue smooth for pretending dry and hardened rims from poking into the wound. Take any cream, you probably carry with you (what matter is that it is fat) and smear it on the wound.

(2) Cover it with a **plaster** with a sterile layer. Take care of the adhesive parts of the plaster getting onto fat-free skin for sticking well.

(3) Next prepare a strip of **broad leucoplast** (5 cm), which will be taped round the heel later on. That means: cut off a bigger item.

(4) Next up is the most important! Take a strip of the **thin foam** *(see tip: Prophylactic Measures against Blisters – Toes/heel)* and fanfold it several times until you get a nice stuffed package. The blister with the overlaid plaster should be covered completely and broad with the pad. Note, that the pad looks a bit thick at first, but will be compressed more and more during the next walking kilometers. Find the most suitable thickness of the stuffing by trial and error. Finally, it depends on how it will fit into the shoe.

(5) The foam stuffing will be fixed to the foot by the prepared strip of leucoplast.

(6) Cut a second strip of leucoplast and tape it right-angled to the first one round the foot. Looks as if you are a victim of the bubonic plague, but it works.

I always did it that way to renew the "bandage" every 4-5 days and keeping fresh air to the thing overnight. Sometimes the foam stuffing can be re-used hereby. The proper healing up must be done after returning home.

It is no problem to wade with this bandage. Can be got wet – the leucoplast blocks nearly everything. As long as the glue remains – hurray: never touch a running system!

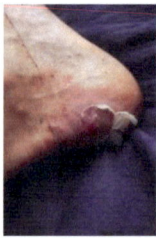 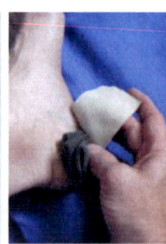 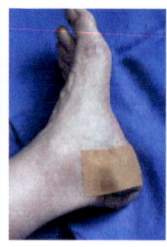 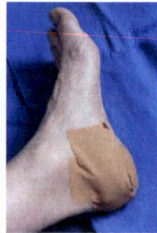

...just till over there!

Those, not having a Sherpa available, who is accompanied by a wardrobe trunk filled with extra clothes, will probably appear with the same outfit on the catwalk of textile indifference for the next 2 or 3 weeks. Due to that one will be enclosed by an aura of aloofness at the end of the journey. Nevertheless, a certain basic hygiene must not be excluded inevitably.

What you can do – and how – for avoiding that bespoke the following tips.

Tip: Toilet Things

Nightmare: the bottle with the shower gel has opened up and the content has poured out into the backpack. You are in luck, if the contaminated area is only a small pouch.

I always use a bar of soap on hiking, right for skin and hair. It can never pour out and in addition to that has a smaller volume than a gel bottle.

Tip: Toilet Paper

Living outdoor does principally mean „back to the roots", but one needs not inevitably approximating the nature people that way to use a specific eating- and faecal-hand during the whole journey. So, external helps are allowed, that are suitable to avoid getting pieces of the great digestion business to the upper extremities or even into the underpants.

Ordinary toilet paper (1-, 2- or n-ply) has a big pack size. The bigger „n" is, the greater is the volume of the paper role. You can eradicate the flaw partially by uncoiling several meters of paper and recoil it very tight and then bring it into the empty core of the role.

How much more elegant is the following variant: **wipes** (there exist ecologically sound ones). Smaller pack size, higher tensile strength, greater hygiene factor and due to a lower viscous drag remarkably friendlier to the body — especially at a time, when you are close to getting an intertrigo.

You don't want to **waste toilet paper**? It works! Grass, leaves or moss not more than arm's length away will serve you well. Moss is the first choice in this affair! The very latest debris can be ignored (and removed later as arse berries) or remaining in the chosen shit position washed away by pouring a well dosed jet of water on one's back in the butt crack.

...just till over there!

Tip: Full-body Ablution

Sooner or later — often sooner — the time has come to wash off sweat and other dirt. Therefore it would seem the thing to plunge into mountain torrents or rivers or lakes.

With a little luck you find a washout, a pit or something similar in the nearby waters close to the camp ground that allows submarining the complete body. Ideally you choose your camp ground against the background of an upcoming bathing unit.

<u>On beforehand</u>: usually the water is freezing-cold and a full-body ablution always is an effort.

Naturally the average length of stay in the water will be very short. Due to that it is recommended to perform the soap scenario on dry ground. Use your drinking cup or a pot for wetting yourself on beforehand.

Use caution in dosing rinsing water for the hair wash: take little doses, otherwise heavy headache threatens due to the coldness of the water.

The culmination is — after being well moistened — to walk valiantly into the „tub" and be slowly completely immersed. Rapid and intermittent breathing supported by cries of enthusiasm motivate to actually finish the dipping process.

You will see, that it is fantastic being once you are in. If you have enough, get out, dry yourself und put on the previously prepared clothes.

Result: One feels totally refreshed and - once being re-dressed — deeply warm.

IMPORTANT: Do ever wear sandals or old shoes while bathing in rivers and lakes. Your feet will quickly lose any feeling in the ice-cold water, what might increase danger of injuries due to the stony riverbeds.

...just till over there!

Tip: Going for a Pee and the Other Thing

What men can do in between without dropping the backpack, means a bit more physical play for women and is simultaneously an additional mosquito trap (see below).

The other excretory function of usually non-liquid matter is mainly distinguished by the permanent absence of sedate white, ergonomically shaped ceramic. This makes for thinking about various techniques for keeping clay like fallout from the internal space of your trousers on one hand and from avoiding muscle cramps in your thighs on the other:

1) <u>The common crouch.</u> Basically you can use it everywhere, but one should keep an eye on the configuration of the ground. If you are, for example in the middle of a field of slippy rocks, the stability could be endangered; too tall vegetation — say in a willow belt — could be inconvenient, too.

2) <u>Leaning against a rock.</u> Depending on duration, this method requires strong thighs. Those are held horizontally, the back is pressed against the rock and now let nature take its course. Do not drop your trousers to low — see key word „fallout" above).

3) <u>Sitting on a big stone.</u> With a little luck you will find a flat rock you can sit on its edge.

4) <u>Thunderbox.</u> In forest areas a fallen tree is a wonderful opportunity. On such opportunities it's a pity, that one cannot do it ahead...

Economize your consumption of paper (*see above; TIP: Toilet Paper*) and do not spread it over a wide area. It would be great to cover your legacy with a stone or earth or even mix it. Stones are everywhere around you. Follow up wanderers and local microorganisms would be thankful for that.

<u>Note:</u>

All mentioned techniques require denudation of relevant parts of the body → *see also Tip: Mosquitos and Defecation.*

...just till over there!

As there are only a few bridges in Sarek it is very probable to face the situation to be forced to cross a watercourse by another method – or rather: track through. According to rumors, there seem to be bridgeless watercourses in other hiking areas, too. The following is the same for those.

Tip: Wading

If you are in luck and the water level is low and/or the watercourse is shallow, the trek can be continued without the forced interruption due to changing shoes by hopping from stone to stone. Otherwise wading is inevitable.

Basic rules:

* <u>never wade barefooted.</u> There is a high risk for deadened feet (due to the coldness of the water) getting hurt in stony waterbeds or by rocks carried away by the strong current. Old sport shoes, trekking sandals or surf shoes or something similar are a good choice.

* latest, if the depth of the water is more than half a calf, use a <u>hiking stick</u> as third leg – rather: use two of them (and get them to full length).

* if the depth is too great (reaching the butt), look for a flatter ford; otherwise the water-pressure will be too high.

* observe changes of the water level during the day; in the morning the level is usually lower than later in the day.

* passing greater rocks it is much better looking for safe footing *between* them than *on* them (slippery when wet).

* open chest and waist belt of the backpack for getting quickly the belts off – in case of falling into knee-deep water it could be difficult to stand up again with a heavy load on the back.

How To

Wade angular to the streaming with the breast against it. Using 2 hiking sticks you always have 3 fixed points (2 feet, 1 stick), which provide a sturdy footing even in strong current. Using only one stick you will always be in a waggly situation. The second stick — pointed upstream - probes the ground, will be set and put weight onto, when the downstream pointed stick will be relocated resp. when the next step will be done.

If you are in doubt, it is better to turn back or to replan the route than to run needless risks.

...just till over there!

An open campfire is a highly romantic thing and in connection with an outdoor stay offers feelings of freedom and adventure. Homelike fiery glow as well as eye-biting smoke support this feeling.

For having a thrilling experience for oneself but no far-reaching for the environment, some basic hints should be taken into account:

Tip: Fire

Open fire — is principally not welcome in the national parks. Due to risk of fire on one hand - at least in the woods — and due to the impact on the surrounding landscape. It is a fact, that it will take many years before a fireplace will be overgrown again.

Avoid open fire for cooking reasons — you carry a cooker with you for that purpose.

In <u>forest areas</u>, along the marked paths there are not many possibilities to raise your tent due to the surface conditions. If there exists a proper camp ground, it will be heavily frequented by wanderers. You will usually find a well prepared fireplace here, ready for use.

In the <u>fjäll</u> the topic „fire" becomes nearly superfluous, because only little burning material can be found there. Above the treeline you have to spend long time for collecting enough burning material (dead twigs and branches from willows or juniper bushes) to start a fire and maintain it afterwards.

In the <u>transitional zone</u> between forest and fjäll often prevails closely covered soil with moss and low shrubs. For starting a fire here without leaving any traces, the recommended procedure is to cut off a proper rectangle for the fireplace with the knife in the ground and roll the surface up like a carpet. Thus, you can kindle directly on the soil without destroying the vegetation. When you are going to leave the camp ground and all is well extinguished, simply unroll the opened plant carpet.

Take only things lying on the ground for burning material. Do not take twigs or branches from living trees!

The best firestarter is filmy ripped off bark from birch trees — ideally taken from deadwood, because living trees are not allowed to be damaged. A handful of it serves as a nest for embers, put some thin scrubs thereon and then a bit thicker twigs up to little branches. Now light the fire. The filmy bark will burn away very fast, so you need to be prepared with enough burning material at your side for feeding the fire and keep it burning.

...just till over there!

Salami roasted on a Spit

...just till over there!

There are legends and myths about the blood thirstiest creature in the Far North: the **mosquito**.

At the height of summer, the hellish breed has its heyday and in this period of time the term „heavenly hosts" must be re-defined. When it gets warm, the suckers indeed are numerous, but actually they are far from covering whole Lapland as a black wafting mass.

Nevertheless they are a nuisance and sometimes are a pain in the arse that one tends to chuck it all in

In addition to that note: where there is wind, you will usually not be molested by that critters.

> In the evening, a little before the sun went down, I was assailed by such multitudes of gnats as surpass all imagination. They seemed to occupy the whole atmosphere, especially when I travelled through low or damp meadows. They filled my mouth, nose and eyes, for they took no pains to get out of my way. Luckily they did not attack me with their bites or stings, though they almost choked me. When I grasped at the cloud before me, my hands were filled with myriads of these insects, all crushed to pieces with a touch, and by far too minute for description. The inhabitants call them Knort, or Knott.
>
> [Linné, pg. 209]

Tip: Quack Remedies for Mosquito Fighting

Nothing helps for an unlimited period of time — this is sad but true. In particular, when one sweats tremendously. Middle European products — and that is my opinion — only put the critters on drugs and stimulate them excessively.

The best advice is to use local products. Nordic Summer, a paste, going around with a smell of burning — was classified as harmful by someone and therefore is out of stock everywhere. Currently MYGGA is on all skins: it is available as spray and stick. Keeps the fleabags at distance, at least for a short while.

Tip: Keeping-Mosquitos-Away-Socks

If you can find some anywhere: procure socks mosquitos cannot bite through. Put them on at the end of a day's walk, when the sheltering hiking shoes are torn off the feet. That will protect you from numerous bites.

Alternatively you can craft keeping-mosquitos-away-foot-containers out of carry-on items belonging to the freezer bag group: feet in, trouser legs closed — ready. The only downside is: due to the hermetic sealing it is fermenting heavily inside the bags. Therefore be careful while putting them off: not too close to the fire and far away from your own nose!

Tip: Keeping Calm in Mosquito Assaults

Hectically waving your hands around, even if you stuck in the center of a cloud of flying aggressors, achieves nothing. A certain number of bites are unavoidable in any case. It is always better to concentrate on head and neck-area as particularly important zones.

Tip: Carry-on Walking despite of Mosquito Clouds

„Who brakes loses!" This motto could come from the mosquitos. Of course there are always some around the wanderer like sputniks, but the cloud formation with the wanderer as its center always starts in the moment, he stops walking. But in this case immediately.

...just till over there!

Tip: Mosquitos inside the Tent

Unavoidable while raising the tent: mosquitos enter the inner tent. When all the fuss is stored, the inner tent needs to be decontaminated. Firstly, eliminate all visible probosics bearer sitting at the „tent-sky". That means, erase them permanently: catch them in the flight and clench your fist for crushing the buzzing enemy; get them moving from the tent sides and wipe them out by clapping your hands or see the single target, fix it between thumb and pointer and bray it with relish. Wipe down the black goo of the mosquito corpses anywhere — don't be shy, hundreds will be added!

Next fluff up all things in the inner tent for getting hidden bloodsuckers move. Deal with them the same way as described above. After each visit to the bushes or other activities the mosquito net had been opened for, start the decontamination from the beginning.

Tip: Mosquito Net (for the Head)

It makes sense in forest and swamp areas. But it is a question whether you like it or not. Some people might feel disabled in their visual perception and due to that may come to stumble and fall. One ought to try it.

<u>Sub-Tip:</u> If you like to drink, there is no need to fold up the net. You can drink right through it. Possibly stuck water droplets in height of the mouth can easily be blown away. Only spontaneous spitting out semisolids should be avoided.

Tip: Mosquitos and Defecation

Before presenting the lurking breed his naked back as a target, you should this and adjacent areas, which will inevitably be freely accessible, precautionally soak with a remedy: either while still being inside the tent or as fast as possible when being outside, as your pants are down.

There is no need to say that the period of time for the subsequent business should be minimized.

...just till over there!

Tip: Mosquitos and Keeping Still

Youngest results in mosquito research say: once the beast has bitten and is still sucking your blood — do not chase it away or wipe it out instantly, but wait until the monster is ready with that.

Reason: by means of its trunk, the mosquito injects proteins in the skin, that prevent blood coagulation. Thus, the mosquito trunk will not be blocked while sucking. The proteins cause an allergic reaction and so-called histamine will be released, which is involved in the defense of foreign substances in the body and causes the itching. The mixture of blood and protein will be removed while sucking. For this purpose you should give the mosquito time to finish its business.

Chasing away or killing the insect early, parts of the proteins will remain in your body and cause the described reactions.

Tip: Recommendation of the Laps

And what does the average Lap do against the mosquitos? Well, nothin'!

His tip is as follows: „The pain derives from inside your head."
Thus, it is all imagination. What a luck!

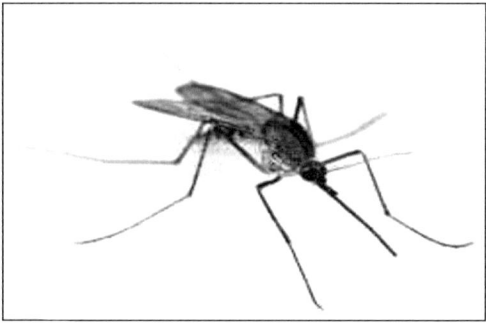

...just till over there!

Hiking trips in the wilderness have one thing in common: there are no signposts to the next hot-dog stand or to somewhere similar. That is the same in Sarek Nationalpark. For that reason it is enormously important to learn all constellations of the northern night sky by heart and be able to determine the North Star instantly at any time.

Otherwise you will be beyond recovery in the northern vastnesses...
→*OF COURSE, THIS IS COMPLETE NONSENSE!* ←

For one thing in summer it never gets dark in Lapland and for another thing, those who wander by night are truly pretty stupid anyway.

Tip: Navigation

Map and compass will be quite sufficient. From my own experience with the Swedish maps I can say, that you are able to run well by only using them. During my hiking trips I was forced only once to use the compass, when I was surprised by suddenly gathering fog.

Nevertheless, you should have learned how to handle the compass before departure.

GPS is nice to have, but not really needed and it steals your feeling to make it in the wild by your own.

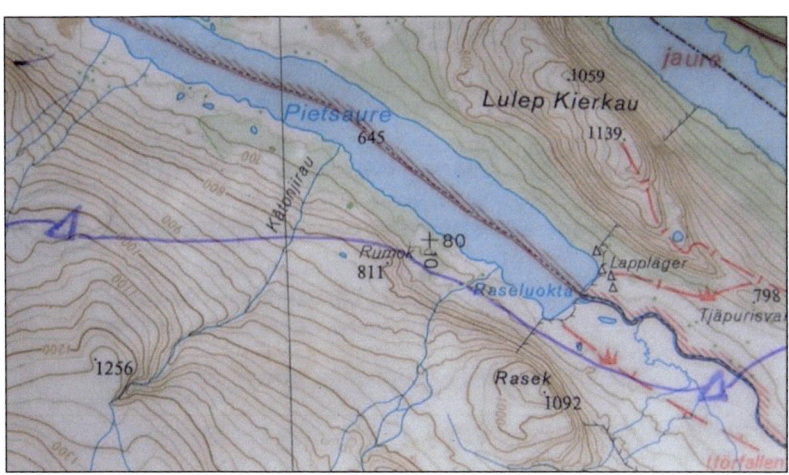

Example of Nya Fjällkartan (Scale 1:100000)

...just till over there!

Going on a journey of this kind, you need one or another item of equipment. Stable footwear and backpack are a must. The same is valid for tent and sleeping bag, if you're gonna stay outside the huts.

In addition to that besides functional clothing, many details have to be considered, that might be useful up to indispensable in many situations. I do not offer a list here. According to that topic one can bustle ad nauseam in the worldwideweb while preparing the journey.

My personal list can be looked up on my official website www.longdistancetrekker.jimdo.com.

Tip: Equipment

You will not find concrete tips to single items of equipment here. The supply in this area is too rich and the number of outdoor shops too great and the personal preferences too various.

The only recommendation from my side is: do not cheap out on shoes, tent and backpack. All other things are of second rank. There is no need for in-brands, especially concerning clothes. Used army trousers will serve you as well. Thus, you can complete your equipment step by step over several years.

Consider, you will be far off any civilizing infrastructure. In the few towns it will probably be possible to pay with plastic money – the great fjäll stations may be exceptions from that rule. Furtheron this luxury will be finished and the golden rule is: cash is king. The country buses principally offer credit card payment, but the machine could be out of order. I actually made this experience.

Tip: Cash

The fjäll stations and Sami settlements usually only accept cash for provisions and art handicraft. This is valid, too, for private boat transfers over lakes, where the STF has installed rowing boat stations for the tough wanderers. Local Sami businessmen often supply motorboat transfers here. Or you are forced to buy that service, because there is no other possibility – e.g. in the Rapadelta. There, Lennart, the Expensive, brings wanderers from the edge of the Sarek Nationalpark to Aktse and vice versa..

...just till over there!

Experts disagree on this question: how to packing the tent? Folded carefully or stuffed chaotically? I think the latter for more senseful and handle my tent the same way as I treat my sleeping bag.

Tip: Stuffing the Tent

A good tent you can rely on in rainy days usually costs a good deal of money. Due to that the one or the other does not like to treat the precious piece seemingly loveless. Indeed, stuffing actually is better than folding; i.e. keep the stuff bag open with one hand and cram the tent merciless with the other hand therein. Even, if it is completely wet.

It is faster on one hand and more advantageous for the tent's lifetime. Folds cause sharp bends and herewith predetermined weak spots for penetrating rainwater.

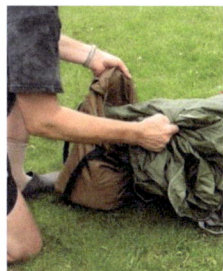 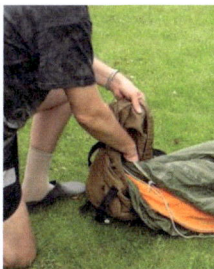 

The extent of clothes in the backpack will be in a narrow frame due to considering of weight and volume. That means: one set of clothing is at the body, and the **one other** inside the backpack for means of replacement in case of would have been getting wet all over.

Tip: Spare Clothing

Pack spare clothing into waterproof plastic bags. Thus, a set of clothes will remain dry even in case of drenching rain and leaky backpack sleeve or even falling off into deep water.

Extract the air while packing the plastic bags shortly before sealing them. This will reduce the packing volume and avoids unplanned bursting of the bags on compressing.

...just till over there!

Who wants to eat and drink warm things needs a cooker and related vessels. The most widespread device in Scandinavia is the Trangia-storm cooker, to be operated with denatured alcohol. Alternatively there are gas cookers or gasoline stoves. Denaturated alcohol (T-Röd Bränsle) can usually be bought in provisions shops of fjäll stations. Concerning gas cartridges it could become tight and gasoline is – according to my own experiences – not available there.

Tip: Transporting Denaturated Alcohol

Who can call his own an alcohol stove, has to tranport the fuel, too. In my opinion SIGG-bottles are particularly suitable for this purpose: they are stable, light, space-saving and secure. In addition to that the bottle with the classic twist-lock has the advantage being not obliged to twist it completely off. Half the way out, there are two little holes located opposite each other that enable controlled outpouring. In newer versions the holes are replaced by longitudinal grooves. The simple aluminium version is available in different sizes (from 0,3 to 1,5 l).

The above mentioned cooker (Trangia) serves in compact form with 2 pots, 1 kettle and a pan together with a burner. I recommend to buy a second burner for a few Euros (simply as a spare one or for extending the cooking time interruption-free).

Important hint: do not refill the hot burner with fuel! It might cause a flash fire.

The preparation of the most dehydrated menus demands to mix powdered nourishment with water. The best method to achieve a lump-free result is the usage of a wire whip.

Tip: Kitchenware – Wire Whip

A **mini wire whip** (costs 1 or 2 Euros) is a tool not measurable with gold for producing culinary delights from dehydrated components, which should be mixed ideally lump-free with water The thing in itself is small, doesn't weigh much and provides incredible benefit.

...just till over there!

The question remains as to how removing the marks of gluttony the best way. There are indeed more comfortable works than cleaning pots and pans after an opulent meal. Usually the choice of kitchenware is poor and thus, there will probably be more often leavings of burnt food in the pots.

> (...)They washed their dishes with their fingers, squirting water out of their mouths upon the spoon (...)
>
> [Linné, p. 293]

Tip: Washing Pots and Pans

Although, there is no need to carry one thing though the wilderness: detergents. It is harmful for the environment and will not have much of an effect. It is better to make use of nature itself and rub the dish objects with moss and mud or sand. That does work tremendously.

Dishwasher with Eco-Rinse

Appendix

Epilog

As Sarek itself – except effects of climate catastrophe – as well as its general image has principally not changed during recent years, I do it the same with a general epilog, which has not changed after 2 earlier travel reports from this geographical region and add it here unchanged.

Let me say a word about the demystification of the SAREK. The desire to hike in this special park existed already since a longer time and this year 2012 welcomed me for the fourth time. I must confess that some insider-reports, at the end of which the reader wonders how the protagonist could survive lots of life-threatening situations actually had a deterrent effect. Nowadays the internet has turned the world into a global village and therefore the sources of information are legion. It has turned out that there are basically two manners of presenting a Sarek trekking tour: the first one puts the focus on the beauty of the experienced nature, whereas the second one takes the same line as the official Swedish scare tactics concerning hiking in the Sarek *(see extracts on pg. 136ff)*.

I know Kungsleden, Padjalantaleden, the Borderpath of Troms, parts of the area south of Torneträsk round Lapporten and the Norwegian Jotunheimen from my own experience – and I dare say that the terrain in Sarek does not put more or less demands on the trained wanderer than other hiking areas.

The great difference is that there are no comforts in form of fjäll stations or waymarks in the Sarek. But even the latter is to put into perspective. Waymarks actually will not be renewed. Anyhow you will find here and there cairns installed by wanderers or faded color markings from bygone days.

In addition to that it is nearly impossible getting irretrievably lost, if you only have a rough map with you. As one can follow the valleys in any case, the approximate direction is given by nature. And there always will be well visible paths, since the soil is soft enough (e.g. in Rapdalen).

The reason for making a tour, which is longer than 5-7 days strenuous is the complete absence of fjäll stations. Thus, some parts of the equipment (tent, sleeping bag, cooker...) become indispensable. Moreover – and this is the important point – any provisions must be dragged along, a weight component that increases with every additional planned day of marching.

...just till over there!

If you are going to equip yourself responsibly, the list of provisions is the only possibility to make drastic cuts. Less provisions means less weight. Less provisions also means less to eat. And less to eat can lead to lesser reserves of power. There is no universal solution from this dilemma. Everyone has to find one by himself.

And how wild is this wilderness actually? Is it the truth being in the Sarek far away from any help? Indeed, there are no official fjäll stations, but still there is a help telephone in the center of the park and some bridges cross the one or other wide river. You are not forced to cross rivers like a pioneer. Nevertheless you can't help wading sometimes.

I think there are more dangerous situations in road traffic than on a hiking tour. Bad situations may occur anyway, that's not the question. A physical defect can be of vital importance, if you are alone. But being on tour with a comrade the undamaged one may reach the help telephone by a maximum of three (forced) day marches.
Note, that mobile phones usually DO NOT work, except in near surrounding of big stations or Sami settlements.

Nonetheless, the Sarek national park provides beautiful sceneries, breathtaking panoramas, impressing rock massifs and glaciers, an adorable outdoor-atmosphere – or in short:

who likes moving in extensive nature waiving civilization-related signs, will reach his full senses here. I look forward to the next „expedition" to the far north.

...just till over there!

In conclusion and for scaring away...

*The following text is provided by the **National Environment Protection Board** of Sweden (**accentuations** by K.H.):*

The Sarek - Myth and Reality

"I want to go hiking in Sarek", you say. **We**, the administrators of the national park, **hope you know what this involves**.

Sarek is a magnificent **untouched** alpine area with sharp peaks and glaciers. Between the mountain massifs there is a network of deeply cut valleys with swift streams. In other words, the terrain is **physically demanding** for the would-be hiker. Sarek is a wilderness **without roads**. The central sections of the national park are many kilometers from inhabited areas. There are **no touristic facilities established, no trails or cabins** here. The hiker is **in serious trouble** if a major accident occurs.
We want to **warn** you for hiking in Sarek if you are **inexperienced**. You should always have successfully accomplished a fair number of mountain expeditions before you set your sights to Sarek.
(...)
It is true that this area is both one of the country`s most valuable natural areas, as well as one of the **most inaccessible**. Although Sarek is a wilderness area of impressive dimensions, if you really want to be alone you should go to one of the lesser known mountain areas. During the tourist season it is hardly desolate in Sarek.

Perhaps by now you`re feeling a little deceived by the mystique surrounding Sarek. The Swedish mountain region is large. Sarek is only one of its many pearls. But one thing is true, if you want to experience **untouched wilderness** in alpine surroundings then Sarek is a class by itself. And if you want to do this **you have to manage entirely by yourself**.

Conditions in Sarek demand that you can read a map, have the right equipment and not least **the right attitude towards difficulties** like bad weather, flooding streams, fatigue etc, which can never be eliminated despite good planning. You must be able to make changes in plans during the hike, **Sarek is to remain an area where nothing is done to accommodate mountain hiking**. This passage is part of the maintenance plans for the national park.
This unique untouched environment is to be preserved intact. You are free, of course, **to visit Sarek at your own risk**. (...) If you feel ready to meet the conditions posed in this wilderness area then we would like to welcome you to Sarek national park.

(...)

...just till over there!

General Advice

Sarek is large and one needs at least one week to hike through the area. You should consider carefully the equipment you will carry with you. A good tent is essential on a hike through Sarek. Make sure it can weather storms. You must have a warm sleeping-bag and extra warm clothing as sweater, scarf and gloves. Even during summer there can be raw days and snowfall is not that unusual.

Rainproof outer clothing is absolutely necessary. The precipitation in Sarek is very high. Count on rain or overcast skies two out of every three days. Sometimes with a little luck the visitor may see the sun for longer periods, but this can never be taken for granted.

You must also take along a good camp stove and sufficient supplies. Though making open camp-fires is not prohibited it is not encouraged, either. The scars left after campfires are not pretty. Moreover, the need for fuel in the form of wood comes up and this depletes the park vegetation. Make camp-fires only when clothes have to be dried. Regular preparation of food over an open fire is absolutely not to be considered. You should have respect for Sarek, birch bark should never be taken from living trees.

It's unavoidable the gear necessary for hiking in the Sarek is going to be fairly heavy. If your complete gear weighs less than 20 kilograms then you've probably forgotten something essential. The above calculation assumes that you are hiking alone, with two the load would be somewhat lighter.

A hiking stick is useful - but don´t cut one from a living tree.

During the winter Sarek makes even more stringent demands on the visitor. Many narrow valleys, e.g. Lullihvavagge, are subjected to **avalanches** which reach even the bottom of the valley. **Snow storms** are menacing and the lack of overnight cabins means that **only highly experienced mountain specialists** can frequent the area with a reasonable degree of safety during this reason.

Route selection

There are **no hiking trails in Sarek** except where an interregional trail known as the "Kungsleden" (The King's Trail) passes through the southern section of the park for a short stretch. Paths have been beaten, however, along several popular routes.

We are neither able nor inclined to give out in detail suitable hiking routes. No one is capable of giving totally infallible tips on Sarek. Snow conditions and the ware run-off situation varies from year to year. You must make your own choice of routes out in the terrain with the help of a map and good judgement.

The Rapa valley

The Rapa valley is magnificent but hiking there is **no Sunday stroll**. The valley is covered in dense vegetation and even if one follows the well-worn paths on the north side the willow thickets are difficult to pass through, especially if it's raining.

...just till over there!

The path crosses over long stretches of marsh which are wet and muddy. Planks have been put out in places recently to protect them against wear. Nevertheless, the path through the valley is **difficult to traverse**.

We recommend mountain hikers to avoid the lower Rapa valley and to travel north of Skierfe and follow the valleys northern slope up to Alep Vassajajakatj, which can be followed downwards to Rapaselet. This route offers very majestic views which outclass what can be seen from the lower part of the valley. (…)

Cabins

There are no tourist cabins in the Sarek. All the same several houses have been built for the purposes of patrolling, reindeer husbandry and research. Alka and Njatso cabins in the western sections, though actually only small huts, are unlocked and may be used by tourists in need. All other cabins are locked. The few Lapp huts which exist in the area are more or less ruins. Only the one at Tielmaskaite is usable.

Tenting sites

It's possible to find good tenting sites nearly everywhere except the highest alpine tracts. High altitude areas with poorer possibilities for camping include the Luttalako plateau and such valleys as Lullihavagge, Jeknavagge and Neitarieppevagge.

Difficult river crossings

Many of Sarek`s streams and rivers are impossible to cross during high water periods. Even small easily-waded streams can overflow their banks and create a strong current. The flow of water in the glacial streams varies greatly depending on the melting rate. They are often narrow, steep and with powerful rapids. Rolling boulders are a particular risk in these streams, a number of Sarek`s rivers are considered **difficult at the best of times**. They include the **Rapaätno, Njatsosjakka, Katokjakka** and **Kukkesvaggejakka** rivers. These are large waterways which the visitor should not tackle. However, the last two do have bridges which can be used for passage. Below mount Laddepakte there is a well-known wading crossing on the Rapaätno, Tielmavadet. Regardless of this it is still arduous to cross the river which even in a normal state is wide and fairly deep here.

Other strategically situated rivers which are often crossed but should be approached with care include:

Sarvesjakka difficult in the lower sections during high water but can be jumped over at a narrow canyon below Ritatjakka river, particularly the section of the canyon further upstream.

Kuoperjakka at the end of the Alkavagge valley, wide and stony, moderately difficult wading.

Tjagnarisjakkatj at the Pielaslätten (plateau) which is sometimes covered by snowdrift, but even otherwise should be approached **with great caution**.

...just till over there!

Palkatjakka in the Njatsosvagge river which is a **treacherous stream** depending on the flow of water.

For your own safety try to keep the number of wadings/crossings at a minimum. During the late summer the flow of water is usually lower in most rivers as long as bad weather hasn't added extra precipitations.

<u>Bridges</u>
There are 12 bridges in Sarek. They have been erected primarily for the sake of reindeer raising. A few are there in connection with the Kungsleden trail, which passes briefly through Sarek. The bridges are marked on the most recent mountain maps. It is possible that one of them **may be damaged** during the winter or spring thaw but the occurrence is rare. The Skarja bridge in the centre of Sarek is taken away just before the onset of winter and is subsequently flown back when conditions permit, usually in June. To get reliable up-to-date information you can call the Mountain Unit (Fjällenheten) in Jokkmokk.

(All things mentioned here, are principally true. The most interesting thing here is the wording. K.H.)

...just till over there!

NILS-ASLAK VALKEAPÄÄ, known as *Áillohaš* in the Northern Sami language (23 March 1943 – 26 November 2001) was a Finnish Sami writer, musician and artist. He was born in Enontekiö in Lapland province, Finland. He lived most of his life in Käsivarsi, close to the border of Sweden, and also in Skibotn in Norway. Valkeapää was born to a family of traditional reindeer herders, but was trained as a school teacher. His most well-known international debut was when he performed at the opening ceremony of the 1994 Winter Olympic Games in Lillehammer, Norway.

The traditional Sami singing of the joik was important in his music, as well as in his painting and in written works. He was first recognized as an artist for his joik during the 1960s, with his first recording Jojkuja from 1968, which contained modernized joik. Valkapeää wrote the music to the motion picture *Ofelaš*, internationally known as *The Pathfinder* in 1987, which was directed by Nils Gaup.

As a writer, he mainly wrote in Sami with his work translated into other languages and eventually published eight collections of poems. One of his best known is Beaivi áhčážan which has been translated to English, titled The Sun, My Father.

Nils-Aslak Valkeapää died on his way home from Japan during a stay in Helsinki at the age of 58. The possible cause of death was from complications from a 1996 automobile accident.

Posthumous publication of Nils-Aslak Valkeapää's work includes two poems included on his godson Niko Valkeapää's eponymous début album. An article published by the Music Information Center Norway stated, "In his trademark, understated style, Niko composes melodies that weave their way into and out of his godfather's words. Nils Aslak Valkeapää was one of the foremost exponents of Sami art and culture through his long and distinguished career as a poet, composer and artist. Says Niko on his godfather's influence: 'I can't deny that Nils Aslak was a role model for me – he was a figure that I would look up to. He has been a source of inspiration and I have included two of his poems on my album to pay homage to him."

...just till over there!

CARL VON LINNÉ, (23 May 1707 – 10 January 1778), was a Swedish botanist, physician, and zoologist, who laid the foundations for the modern biological naming scheme of binomial nomenclature. He is known as the father of modern taxonomy, and is also considered one of the fathers of modern ecology. Many of his writings were in Latin, and his name is rendered in Latin as Carolus Linnæus.

Rudbeck had made a journey to Lapland in 1695, but the detailed results of his exploration were lost in a fire seven years afterwards. Linnaeus' hope was to find new plants, animals and possibly valuable minerals. He was also curious about the customs of the native Sami people, reindeer-herding nomads who wandered Scandinavia's vast tundras. In April 1732, Linnaeus was awarded a grant from the Royal Society of Sciences in Uppsala for his journey.

Linnaeus began his expedition from Uppsala in May; he travelled on foot and horse, bringing with him his journal, botanical and ornithological manuscripts and sheets of paper for pressing plants. Near Gävle he found great quantities of Campanula serpyllifolia, later known as Linnaea borealis, the twinflower that would become his favorite. He sometimes dismounted on the way to examine a flower or rock and was particularly interested in mosses and lichens, the latter a main part of the diet of the reindeer, a common and economically important animal in Lapland.

Linné's book „The Lapland Journey: Iter Laponicum" is a travel diary, which has never been tidied up by himself. Due to this, the work is written in a briskly direct and unaffected manner, quasi saying openly what came into his head.

Linné's Laplandbook was published for the first time in England in 1811 – nearly 80 years after the end of the journey. It took another 80 years, when the first edition in Swedish language was published in 1889 (111 years after his death).

Linnaeus' last years were troubled by illness. He had suffered from a disease called the Uppsala fever in 1764, but survived thanks to the care of Rosén. In December 1777, he had a third stroke which greatly weakened him, and eventually led to his death on 10 January 1778 in Hammarby.

...just till over there!

KNUT HAMSUN *4 (August 4, 1859 – February 19, 1952) was a Norwegian author, who was awarded the Nobel Prize in Literature in 1920. Hamsun's work spans more than 70 years and shows variation with regard to the subject, perspective and environment. He published more than 20 novels, a collection of poetry, some short stories and plays, a travelogue, and some essays.

The young Hamsun objected to realism and naturalism. He argued that the main object of modern literature should be the intricacies of the human mind, that writers should describe the "whisper of blood, and the pleading of bone marrow". Hamsun is considered the "leader of the Neo-Romantic revolt at the turn of the [20th] century", with works such as Hunger (1890), Mysteries (1892), Pan (1894), and Victoria (1898). His later works—in particular his "Nordland novels"—were influenced by the Norwegian new realism, portraying everyday life in rural Norway and often employing local dialect, irony, and humor.

Hamsun is considered to be "one of the most influential and innovative literary stylists of the past hundred years" (ca. 1890–1990). He pioneered psychological literature with techniques of stream of consciousness and interior monologue, and influenced authors such as Thomas Mann, Franz Kafka, Maxim Gorky, Stefan Zweig, Henry Miller, Hermann Hesse, and Ernest Hemingway. Isaac Bashevis Singer called Hamsun "the father of the modern school of literature in his every aspect—his subjectiveness, his fragmentariness, his use of flashbacks, his lyricism. The whole modern school of fiction in the twentieth century stems from Hamsun". Ernest Hemingway stated that "Hamsun taught me to write".

Knut Hamsun died on February 19, 1952, aged 92, in Grimstad.

ROBERT CROTTET, (November 23, 1908 – May 04, 1987) was born in St. Petersburg, was Swiss Citizen with French language. He often flew from our latitudes, habits and restraints and e.g. was wandering through Lapland, describing his experiences in travel books.

ERNEST ESTLIN CUMMINGS, (October 14, 1894 – September 3, 1962), known as **E. E. Cummings**, with the abbreviated form of his name often written by others in lowercase letters as **e e cummings** (in the style of some of his poems), was an American poet, painter, essayist, author, and playwright. His body of work encompasses approximately 2,900 poems, two autobiographical novels, four plays and several essays, as well as numerous drawings and paintings. He is remembered as an eminent voice of 20th century poetry.

...just till over there!

<u>Sami names for places</u>

The Sami names for places are mainly used from the Three-Country-Point down to the northern Jämtland.

All these names were derived for practical reasons. Men were forced to identify and localize topographic objects and locations. The names contain words, that characterize the place or tell the event happening at a certain time or give the name of a settler or something like that.

The Sami names contain words specific for the conditions the Sapmi live in, e.g. there are several names for mountain ranges with different meanings: cohkka (tjåkka) for mountain top, gaisi (kaise) for steep high mountain regions or oaivi (åive) for a head-shaped mountain. Many names cannot be translated, but need totally different expressions. Thus, they cannot be described with a single word.

<u>Short and simplified rules for pronunciation</u>

á	= long A in "marvelous"
å	= as long O in "more"
o	= as O in "shot"
u	= as U
c, z	= as tz in "Ritz"
č, ž	= as tsch in "chain"
š	= as sch in "shirt"

In the umlauts ea, ie, oa and uo both vocals will be spoken.

...just till over there!

Usual Sami topographic terms.

Due to dialectical reasons they might be written in different ways. Find here the most often used spellings.

áhpi, ape	great swamp
bákti, pakte	steep cliff
coalmi, tjålme	strait
cohkka, tjåkkå	mountain top
corru, tjärro	mountain back
eatnu, ätno	great river, stream
gáisi, kaise	steep high mountain region
gorsa, kårså	canyon, narrow valley
jávri, jaure	lake
jávrras, jaurati	small lake
jeaggi, jägge	swamp
jietnja, jiekna	ice, glacier
johka, jåkkå	creek, river
láhku, lako	highly situated, wide heath
luokta	bai
luoppal	small inland lake
luspi, luspe	place, where a river comes out of a lake
njárga, njarka	peninsula
njunni, njunnje	foothills of a fjäll
oaivi, åive	head-shaped mountain
riehppi, rieppe	niche-shaped valley, often with a glacier hard-to-reach
sáiva, salva	lake
savvun, savon	standing water
skáldi, skaite	tongue of land between two waters
suolu, suolo	island, small island
vággi, vagge	valley, U-shaped valley
varas, varatj	small mountain range
várdu, vardo	low mountain range with panorama point
varri, vare	mountain, mountain range

...just till over there!

Mostly used adjectives for determination of the position

ailip, alep	western, higher
allmus, alem us	most west, highest
lulip, lulep	more east
lulimus, lulemus	most east
bajip, pajep	over, higher
bajimus, pajemus	on top
vuolip, vuolep	lower

Provisions in fjäll stations

This is a basic fund that may vary dependent on how big a station is. In bigger stations the fund may be extended.

canned meat or fish
soups, canned meals
instant soups
strong broth
canned veggies
beans, different kinds
corn
canned fruits
instant cream

Other food:
potatoe puree
ricel
noodles

Adventure Food:
oat flakes
spread
chees in tubes
salami
knackwurst
orange jam

applesauce
stewed cranberries
Ketchup/moustard
sugar
salt
bread and cookies
crips bread
chocolate
coffee
tea
milk powder
sweets
Snacks/dry fruits
raisins
toiletries
toilet paper
gas
spiritus, T-röd bränsle
matches
mountain maps

...just till over there!

Find here **a list of mountains in Sweden** containing 12 tops that are higher than 2000 meters:

Rank	Mountain Top	Province	Height
1.	Kebnekaise, Sydtoppen	Lapland	2104 m
2.	Kebnekaise, Nordtoppen	Lapland	2097 m
3.	Sarektjåkkå, Stortoppen	Lapland	2089 m
4.	Kaskasatjåkka	Lapland	2076 m
5.	Sarektjåkkå, Nordtoppen	Lapland	2056 m
6.	Kaskasapakte	Lapland	2043 m
7.	Sarektjåkkå, Sydtoppen	Lapland	2023 m
8.	Akka, Stortoppen	Lapland	2016 m
9.	Akka, Nordvästtoppen	Lapland	2010 m
10.	Sarektjåkkå, Buchttoppen	Lapland	2010 m
11.	Pårtetjåkkå	Lapland	2005 m
12.	Palkattjåkkå	Lapland	2002 m

...just till over there!

RESOURCES

Robert Crottet, *Verzauberte Wälder*, dtv 1984, [Crottet1]

Robert Crottet, *Am Rande der Tundra*, Fischer Taschenbuch Verlag, April 1980, [Crottet2]

E. E. Cummings, *Complete Poems 1904-1962*. Ed. George J. Firmage. New York: Liveright, 1991

Knut Hamsun, *Sämtliche Romane und Erzählungen*, Bd. 1, List Verlag 1977, [Hamsun]

Carl von Linné, *Lachesis Lapponica or a Tour in Lapland, White and Cochrane, London 1811, Volume I*[Linné1]

Carl von Linné, *Lachesis Lapponica or a Tour in Lapland, White and Cochrane, London 1811, Volume II* [Linné2]

Nils-Aslak Valkeapää, *The Sun, my Father,* DAT, Guovdageaidnu 1997, [Valkeapää1]

Nils-Aslak Valkeapää, *Trekways of the Wind,* DAT. Guovdageaidnu 1994, [Valkeapää2]

Colored fotos by Niklas Heyne;   b/w-fotos by Klaus Heyne

Data of Nils-Aslak Valkeapää:
http://en.wikipedia.org/wiki/Nils-Aslak_Valkeap%C3%A4%C3%A4

Data of Carl von Linné:
http://en.wikipedia.org/wiki/Carl_von_linne

Data of Knut Hamsun:
http://en.wikipedia.org/wiki/Knut_Hamsun.

Data of E.E.Cummings
http://en.wikipedia.org/wiki/E._E._Cummings

Data of Robert Crottet
http://en.wikipedia.org/wiki/RobertCrottet

Topographic Sami names; overview of fjällstations, etc etc
www.stf.se

...just till over there!

IMPRINT

Title	...just till over there / Klaus Heyne
Person(s)	Heyne, Klaus
Issue	2. Edition.
Publisher	Norderstedt : Books on Demand
Year of Publication	2014
ISBN	9783735778499
Pages/Format	146 pg., 67 Illustr.; 210 mm x 148 mm,
Subject Group	910 Geography, Travels
Date of Publication	September 2014

BIBLIOGRAPHY

JOTUNHEIMEN - Wandern in der Heimat der Riesen
Eine Wanderung in Norwegens Bergwelt
ISBN: **978-3839136485**

Zwei im Sarek:
Wandern unter der Mitternachtssonne
ISBN: **978-3839134092**

Zwei zum ersten Mal im Sarek:
Wandern im Land der Samen
ISBN: **978-3844802054**

Suggestions and critical reviews are welcome.

Please write to: klaus.heyne@web.de
Visit: www.longdistancetrekker.jimdo.com

...just till over there!

MEMOS

...just till over there!